D1425189

sharing sweet secrets
gluten & wheat free

pamela moriarty

photography by Jacqui Way

MURDOCH BOOKS

First published by Pamela Moriarty 2006
www.glutenfreesecrets.com.au

This edition published in 2007 by
Murdoch Books Pty Limited
www.murdochbooks.com.au

Murdoch Books Australia
Pier 8/9
23 Hickson Road
Millers Point NSW 2000
Phone: +61 (0) 2 8220 2000
Fax: +61 (0) 2 8220 2558

Murdoch Books UK Limited
Erico House, 6th Floor
93–99 Upper Richmond Road
Putney, London SW15 2TG
Phone: +44 (0) 20 8785 5995
Fax: +44 (0) 20 8785 5985

Chief Executive: Juliet Rogers
Publishing Director: Kay Scarlett

Editor: Cyndy Nelson
Designer: Lisa Burns
Photographer: Jacqui Way
Project Manager: Anastasia McCall Hammond
Production: Maiya Levitch

Copyright 2007 Pamela Moriarty

All rights reserved. No part of this publication may be
reproduced, stored in a retrieval system or transmitted
in any form or by any means, electronic, mechanical,
photocopying, recording or otherwise, without the prior
written permission of the publisher.

Cataloguing-in-Publication data
National Library of Australia

Moriarty, Pamela.
Sharing sweet secrets : gluten & wheat free.
Includes index.

ISBN 9781741960204 (pbk.).

1. Gluten-free diet - Recipes. 2. Wheat-free diet -
Recipes. I. Title.

641.56318

Printed by 1010 Printing International Limited in 2007.
PRINTED IN CHINA.

IMPORTANT: Those who might be at risk from the
effects of salmonella poisoning (the elderly, pregnant
women, young children and those suffering from immune
deficiency diseases) should consult their doctor with any
concerns about eating raw eggs.

contents

acknowledgements

The generosity of the following people made this book possible.

My husband Kevin who encouraged me to begin writing **sharing sweet secrets gluten and wheat free**. Family and friends who have eaten my food and insisted I "write it down" whenever I have developed a new recipe, thank you.

Special thanks to Helen Jones for always being there, whether it be for her computing skills or assistance in testing and tasting my recipes. Her judgement, calm influence and sense of humour was invaluable.

To Wendy Christophersen for her initial edit, which gave consistency and order to the book.

Thanks also to Robyn Russell, author/publisher of **gluten free and easy,** who unselfishly shared her knowledge and was just an email away when I needed assistance.

Final acknowledgement goes to the enthusiastic professional team - especially photographer Jacqui Way and graphic designer Lisa Burns, who brought all of the elements together to create **sharing sweet secrets gluten and wheat free** and made it such fun along the way!

introduction

Why should everyone else have all the fun? Coeliacs too are hungry, for not only delicious food but for beautiful cookbooks. The perception is that gluten free food is bland and boring. This is just not so. It can be fabulous, fun and funky too.

Desserts and small sweet treats were foods I craved most when I was first diagnosed with Coeliac Disease about 20 years ago. I also have two siblings with the chronic skin disorder Dermatitis Herpetiformis, which has a known relationship to Coeliac Disease. Research has shown that a gluten free diet is essential for people with these conditions. Over many years I have experimented with creating and adapting recipes for gluten free cooking. In fact, most people I cook for eat gluten free food and do not even know it.

When invited to dine with family and friends, they are always concerned about what I can and cannot eat. This book has been written because of their requests to 'write it down' whenever I have developed a new gluten free recipe. Even if you are not a Coeliac, you may know of someone with a wheat or gluten allergy. But remember, you don't have to be a Coeliac to love the food in this book.

I am a passionate cook, having worked in the hospitality industry for approximately 20 years. My professional experience includes a successful catering business, a partnership in a small restaurant and working at Government House in Adelaide.

Eating in restaurants can be a problem for Coeliacs. I have on many occasions become ill from ingesting gluten inadvertently. Many chefs are often unaware that even the smallest amount of gluten is 'poison' for our bodies and can cause a severe reaction. It is important to understand that a gluten free diet is not a fad, but a key factor for good health and well-being for people with Coeliac Disease.

Simply by ensuring the pantry is stocked with gluten free ingredients will make cooking for Coeliacs easy and more importantly, safe. For this reason I have included a general gluten free pantry stock list. To obtain a comprehensive guide to gluten free ingredients and products contact the Coeliac Society in your State. The websites of all State Societies are accessible from the CSA website: www.coeliac.org.au
There are many gluten free products readily available. I shopped locally at the supermarket and central market for all of the ingredients in this book.

I believe that food should be a simple pleasure to prepare. Make good use of your freezer by preparing pastry, tart bases and sponges in advance. With frozen berries and stewed fruits on hand you can have a dessert ready in minutes. I also like to keep gluten free breadcrumbs and cake crumbs in the freezer as there are many desserts in which they are used. A well-stocked pantry means no last minute panic when friends arrive unexpectedly.

The recipes I have chosen range from delicate to generous. They are delicious, stylish and above all simple. Many have 'do ahead' elements, making dessert preparation very manageable for busy people who love to cook. I have simplified long cooking techniques by using the microwave oven for quick results, without compromising the end product.

No longer will you feel deprived especially when it comes to eating sweet foods. I hope you will find my book helpful when choosing a suitable sweet treat or dessert that everyone, not only Coeliacs, can eat. You can now eat like a regular person too!

understanding coeliac disease

a simple explanation

Coeliac Disease (pronounced seel-ee-ack) or Gluten Sensitive Enteropathy produces a number of symptoms resulting from severe inflammation of the small intestine. This occurs when gluten, the sticky insoluble protein found in wheat, barley, oats and rye, is ingested. Damage to the mucous membrane lining and ultimately the destruction of the villi (finger-like projections) occurs.

Coeliac Disease may occur in children but many people are not diagnosed until middle or late life. The symptoms of untreated coeliac disease will gradually get worse. The long-term consequences are those related to poor nutrition and malabsorption of vitamins, minerals and other nutrients. This leads to increased risk of anaemia, osteoporosis, poor growth, infertility or miscarriage. There is a small, but real, increased risk of cancer and small intestinal lymphoma in untreated coeliac disease.

symptoms

The symptoms of Coeliac Disease reflect the consequences of chronic malabsorption and may include the following:
severe diarrhoea, rumbling stomach and flatulence
constipation, bloating and cramping
nausea and vomiting
tiredness and irritability
anaemia - an iron or folic acid deficiency is common
recurrent mouth ulcers
vitamin and mineral deficiencies - calcium, zinc and some B vitamins
bone pain (due to soft bone)
weight loss

diagnosis

The latest blood screening tests is called Transglutaminase antibody, TTG IgA. A positive result should be followed up with a biopsy to confirm Coeliac Disease.

treatment

Strict adherence to a gluten free diet for life.

Note: This is not a medical book. The above information should be used as a guide only. If you are unwell and suspect Coeliac Disease, seek professional advice from a qualified medical practitioner and qualified dietitian.

secrets for success
making and baking gluten free

first and foremost
Read recipe through completely.

Assemble all ingredients.

Weigh out quantities or measure ingredients accurately.

Prepare oven trays or tins for baking.

If using a hand-held electric mixer allow extra time for beating.

Remember to use eggs, butter and liquid at room temperature unless stated to the contrary in the recipe.

Use unsalted butter for sweet food cooking.

Use large eggs for all of the recipes (minimum weight 59g).

Some flours require more liquid than others, so always add liquid a little at a time, err on the side of caution.

Note: I have tried to use less sugar than in conventional recipes but you can add more if you have a sweet tooth.

conventional and fan-forced ovens
Oven temperatures are given as a guide only, as conventional ovens do vary depending on whether gas, electric or fan-forced is used.

microwave ovens
The recipes in my book are designed for microwave ovens with an output of 600 watts. Hence cooking times will vary for microwave ovens with a higher or lower output. I have suggested power levels of HIGH-MEDIUM-LOW. This refers to the output e.g. 600-400-200 watts. Microwave ovens do vary in the description of these output levels. **So get to know your microwave oven.**

bain-marie
Also called a 'water bath', this is a baking pan into which smaller containers (pudding, timbale and dariole moulds) are placed. Hot or boiling water is then poured into the pan to come halfway up the sides of containers. For ease of transferring the pan and its contents to the oven, it is best to put the pan with containers onto the oven shelf and then pour in the hot water. Simply slide the pan back into position in the oven ready for baking. This method of cooking is often used when baking custards and puddings on a low temperature to prevent curdling.

ingredient substitutions
Where oil, melted margarine or melted butter are mentioned you can use any one of these products.

A substitute for buttermilk is 1 cup of milk with 1 tablespoon of lemon juice added. Rest for 5 minutes before using in baking.

Replace buttermilk with yogurt or sour cream.

Whole milk can be substituted with skim milk.

Dry gluten free breadcrumbs may be substituted with stale cake crumbs.

Plain cake or sponge crumbs may be replaced with crumbled savoiardi (sponge fingers).

Baking powder can be prepared by combining 1 teaspoon cream of tartar with ½ teaspoon bicarbonate of soda. This is equal to 2 teaspoons of baking powder.

I have suggested serving most desserts with cream but feel free to substitute thick yogurt, crème fraiche, mascarpone or ice cream depending on the chosen dessert.

Dark choc bits may be substituted with Nestlé's Plaistowe premium dark chocolate (63% cocoa couverture). See melting instructions on the packet. You will need to chop the chocolate pieces if they are to be **folded** into a recipe rather than **melted**.

small sweet treats

'v' indicates variation

almond bread

Light, crisp and nutty, almond bread is a perfect accompaniment with coffee or tea. I also like to serve it with mousse or fools, making these desserts a little more special. For a Christmas treat prepare **pistachio and craisin bread** (see **variation** below). It also makes a delightful gift when wrapped in cellophane and tied with ribbon.

Lightly grease a loaf tin measuring approximately 24cm x 9cm.

preheat oven to 180°C

3 eggs (59g), whites only
½ cup caster sugar
¾ cup gluten free plain flour
¾ cup whole un-blanched almonds

whip egg whites until soft peaks form.

beat in sugar gradually, a tablespoon at a time until dissolved and mixture is firm and glossy.

sift flour and fold in using a low speed or a metal spoon.

add almonds gently turning them through the mixture.

spoon mixture into tin.

bake for about 25 minutes or until light golden brown and firm to the touch. Test with a skewer, which should come out clean.

cool in tin for a few minutes before turning out onto a wire rack.

When almond bread has cooled wrap in foil and refrigerate overnight. The following day cut almond bread into very thin slices using an electric knife. Place slices on oven trays and bake at 110°C for about 25 minutes or until crisp.

cool completely before storing in an airtight container.

variation

pistachio and craisin bread
Follow the recipe above substituting almonds with ½ cup unsalted shelled pistachio nuts. Add ¼ cup craisins after folding in the nuts.

shared secrets
Almond bread keeps well for several weeks stored in an airtight container.

Prepare and bake several loaves of almond bread and freeze. When required defrost a loaf, slice and bake until crisp, as above.

Substitute craisins with chopped dried apricots.

Craisins are sweetened dried cranberries available in supermarkets.

almond biscotti

Biscotti literally means 'twice-baked'. Italians often dip their biscotti into espresso at breakfast time. You can also enjoy this hard biscuit with a glass of Vino Santo or your favourite liqueur.

Makes approximately 40

Line an oven tray with baking paper.

preheat oven to 180°C

1 cup gluten free plain flour
⅓ cup pure icing sugar
1 teaspoon gluten free baking powder
½ cup whole un-blanched almonds
2 eggs (59g)
¼ teaspoon vanilla or almond essence

additional ingredients
1 lightly beaten egg white for glazing

sift flour, icing sugar and baking powder together.

add almonds.

blend eggs and essence together lightly with a fork.

stir egg mixture through flour mixture.

shape dough using dampened hands into two logs measuring 14cm x 6cm.

place logs onto prepared oven tray leaving space between them. Flatten slightly.

glaze with egg white by brushing it over the top of the dough.

bake for 20-25 minutes. Remove from oven and cool for 5-10 minutes.

reduce oven temperature to 140°C.

cut biscotti logs on an angle into 5mm widths, using a serrated or electric knife.

place slices back onto oven tray.

bake a further 20-30 minutes or until biscotti are dry and crisp. Turn slices over once during cooking time.

cool on a wire rack.

store in an airtight container.

shared secrets
Substitute hazelnuts for almonds.
Biscotti keeps well for up to 2 weeks.

chocodamia biscotti

Deliciosa! These 'twice-baked' biscuits keep well or may be eaten immediately. The most well-known biscotti are amaretti. There are many types of biscotti, some with soft centres and others are hard, like this recipe.

Makes approximately 40

Line an oven tray with baking paper.

preheat oven to 180°C

¾ cup gluten free plain flour

¼ cup Dutch style cocoa

1 teaspoon gluten free baking powder

⅓ cup caster sugar

1 tablespoon grated dark chocolate or finely chop 1 tablespoon choc bits

½ cup macadamia nuts

2 eggs (59g)

sift flour, cocoa and baking powder together.

stir in sugar, grated chocolate and nuts.

place eggs into a small bowl and beat gently with a fork.

stir into dry ingredients to form a muddy dough. Keep on working the dry ingredients in, you may think it needs more liquid, but it will come together.

shape dough using dampened hands into two logs measuring 14cm x 6cm.

place logs onto prepared oven tray leaving space between them. Flatten slightly.

bake for 20 minutes. Remove from oven and cool for 5-10 minutes.

reduce oven temperature to 140°C.

cut biscotti logs on a slight angle into 5mm slices using a serrated or electric knife.

place slices back onto oven tray and bake a further 20 minutes or until biscotti are dry. Turn slices over once during cooking time.

cool on a wire rack.

store in an airtight container.

shared secret

Biscotti keeps well for up to 2 weeks.

amaretti biscuits

These wonderful, traditional Italian biscuits are so versatile. There are many desserts in which they are used. Amaretti are great for dunking in coffee. There are soft and hard crunchy amaretti—the following recipe is the soft centre variety.

Makes approximately 20

Line an oven tray with baking paper.

preheat oven to 180°C

¾ cup blanched almonds

½ cup pure icing sugar

1 teaspoon maize cornflour

1 teaspoon amaretto liqueur

2 or 3 drops of almond essence

1 egg (59g), white only

additional ingredients

12 blanched almonds cut in half lengthwise, for decoration

grind almonds, but not too finely, in a food processor.

add icing sugar and cornflour then process for a few more seconds.

add amaretto, almond essence and egg white.

whizz until mixture is blended and looks like a thick, sticky paste.

spoon into a piping bag fitted with a 1.5cm plain nozzle.

pipe small rounds onto baking paper. Hold piping bag about 1cm above the baking paper, squeeze and lift the piping bag away. Use a knife to separate paste from the nozzle.

press half an almond in the centre of each biscuit.

bake for about 15 minutes. Cool for a few minutes before removing to a wire rack.

store in an airtight container.

shared secret

Use the rounded handle of a wooden spoon to push the last of the paste out of piping bag.

chocolate cookies

This is my comfort cookie. It has a soft texture and is ever so moreish.

Makes 18 large or 24 smaller cookies

Line a flat oven tray with baking paper.

preheat oven to 180°C

60g soft unsalted butter

¼ cup caster sugar

1 egg (59g)

¼ cup gluten free plain flour

¼ cup white rice flour

¼ cup maize cornflour

¼ cup Dutch style cocoa

additional ingredients

4 choc bits per cookie to garnish

cream butter and sugar in a food processor. Scrape down sides of processor several times.

add egg and whizz to combine.

add all flours and cocoa then whizz to blend. There is no need to sift these ingredients.

remove dough from food processor.

roll 18 walnut-sized balls or 24 smaller balls and place onto prepared oven tray.

flatten to about 5mm in depth and press choc bits on top of each cookie.

bake for about 15 minutes.

cool on a wire rack. Cookies will continue to firm as they cool.

shared secret
These cookies keep well, stored in an airtight container for several weeks, but only if you don't eat them!

muesli biscuits

When making biscuits I often double the quantity and freeze half of the unbaked mixture. That way it is just a matter of defrosting and baking the stored biscuit mixture, thereby eliminating the preparation and washing up.

Makes approximately 28 biscuits

Line a flat oven tray with baking paper.

preheat oven to 180°C

60g soft unsalted butter

¼ cup caster sugar

1 egg (59g)

1 orange, finely grated zest only

¼ cup gluten free plain flour

¼ cup white rice flour

¼ cup chestnut or buckwheat flour

¼ cup maize cornflour

¼ cup gluten free muesli

⅓ cup almonds, roughly chopped

⅓ cup chopped raisins or dried apricots (optional)

cream butter and sugar in a food processor.

add egg and orange zest then whizz briefly.

add all flours and pulse (turn on and off action) to blend. There is no need to sift the flours.

add muesli, almonds and raisins, pulsing to combine.

scrape mixture onto freezer wrap.

using the freezer wrap, shape mixture into a log 4cm in diameter and lightly mark even cuts along the top. Refrigerate for 10 minutes before cutting.

cut biscuits and place onto prepared tray, reshaping if necessary.

bake for about 20 minutes or until golden brown.

remove biscuits from tray and cool on a wire rack.

shared secrets

These biscuits keep well for several weeks.

Prepare double the quantity of biscuit dough and freeze half for later use.

muffins - apple and pecan

Quick and easy muffins for breakfast, brunch or lunchtime treat.

Makes 8 large muffins or 10 smaller muffins

Grease a muffin tray or insert paper patty pans into muffin holes.

preheat oven to 190°C

1 cooking apple (approximately 170g)
¼ cup pecan nuts, roughly chopped
2 eggs (59g)
¼ cup light vegetable or grapeseed oil
¼ cup apple juice or milk
½ cup gluten free self raising flour
¼ cup maize cornflour
⅓ cup white rice flour
1 teaspoon ground cinnamon
1 teaspoon gluten free baking powder
½ teaspoon bicarbonate of soda
½ cup caster sugar

peel, core and finely dice apple.

combine prepared apple and nuts. Set aside.

place eggs, oil and half of the apple juice into a medium size bowl and whisk lightly.

sift flours, cinnamon, baking powder and bicarbonate of soda together.

stir sugar into flour mixture.

fold liquid into flour mixture using a fork, do not over-stir. Add remainder of apple juice if necessary.

stir combined apple and nuts into the batter.

spoon into muffin tray, filling each hole three-quarters full.

bake for about 25 minutes. Test with a skewer which should come out clean.

cool slightly before removing from muffin tray to a wire rack.

shared secrets

Half-fill any unfilled holes in muffin tray with water. This will assist muffins to cook evenly.

Muffins freeze well.

Freshen muffins in a microwave on Medium for 10-15 seconds per muffin.

Cook muffin mixture in paper patty pans placed in a muffin tray.

muffins - banana & carrot crumble

When that over-ripe banana sits in the fruit bowl and begs to be eaten but isn't, whizz up these fabulous muffins. Serve with a cuppa for breakfast or brunch. Also great for dessert with sliced bananas, **caramel sauce** (page 42) and cream. Yum!

Makes 8 large muffins

Grease a muffin tray or insert paper patty pans into muffin holes.

preheat oven to 190°C

for the crumble

1 tablespoon gluten free plain flour

1 tablespoon unsalted butter

1 tablespoon brown or caster sugar

1 tablespoon roughly chopped walnuts

1 tablespoon shredded coconut

1 tablespoon gluten free muesli or other gluten free cereal

for the muffins

½ cup gluten free self raising flour

¼ cup buckwheat flour

¼ cup white rice flour

1 teaspoon gluten free baking powder

¼ teaspoon bicarbonate of soda

½ teaspoon mixed spice

¼ cup soft brown sugar

⅓ cup walnuts, roughly chopped

⅓ cup light vegetable or grapeseed oil

2 eggs (59g)

1 very ripe banana, peeled and mashed

1 carrot, grated (approximately 130g)

1-2 tablespoons milk, Greek style yogurt or apple juice

for the crumble

place flour into a small bowl.

rub in butter and sugar.

combine with remaining ingredients.

for the muffins

sift flours, baking powder, bicarbonate of soda and mixed spice.

stir in sugar and walnuts.

place oil, eggs, banana and carrot in a bowl and stir with a fork.

fold into flour mixture.

stir in milk or other alternative, only if mixture is too dry.

spoon into muffin tray, filling each hole three-quarters full.

top each muffin with a spoonful of **crumble**.

bake for about 25 minutes. Test with a skewer which should come out clean.

cool slightly before removing from muffin tray to a wire rack.

shared secrets

These muffins freeze well.

Freshen muffins in a microwave for 10-15 seconds per muffin.

Freeze over-ripe bananas to have on hand for baking in cakes or muffins. (Wrap bananas in plastic wrap or foil before freezing.)

muffins - blueberry, buckwheat and lemon

This is a great combination of flavours and such a treat at breakfast or, for that matter, anytime. You could also substitute apples, pears, plums or rhubarb.

Makes 12

Grease a muffin tray or insert paper patty pans into muffin holes.

preheat oven to 190°C

½ cup white rice flour

½ cup gluten free self raising flour

¼ cup buckwheat flour

¼ cup maize cornflour

1 teaspoon gluten free baking powder

125g soft unsalted butter

½ cup caster sugar

1 lemon, grated zest only

3 eggs (59g)

½ cup Greek style yogurt

1 cup blueberries, fresh or frozen

sift flours and baking powder together. Set aside.

cream butter, sugar and lemon zest in the small bowl of an electric mixer until pale and thick.

add eggs one at a time and beat well. Scrape down sides of bowl.

add yogurt and beat to combine.

fold in sifted mixture using a low speed.

add blueberries, gently folding in using a large metal spoon.

spoon into muffin tray.

bake for 25-30 minutes. Test with a skewer which should come out clean.

cool slightly before removing from muffin tray to a wire rack.

shared secrets

Frozen berries may be used straight from the freezer. There is no need to thaw before baking in muffins, cakes or tarts.

These muffins freeze well.

Freshen muffins in a microwave on Medium for 10-15 seconds per muffin.

muffins - chocolate buttermilk

If you need a quick chocolate fix it is hard to go past these decadent muffins. Freeze some to have on hand for when that craving hits.

Makes 12 large muffins

Grease a muffin tray or insert paper patty pans into the muffin holes.

preheat oven to 190°C

¼ cup gluten free self raising flour

¼ cup white rice flour

½ cup maize cornflour

½ cup Dutch style cocoa

1 teaspoon gluten free baking powder

½ teaspoon bicarbonate of soda

125g unsalted butter, cubed

¾ cup caster sugar

2 eggs (59g)

½ cup buttermilk (approximately)

additional ingredients
4 choc bits per muffin to garnish

sift flours, cocoa, baking powder and bicarbonate of soda together. Set aside.

cream butter and sugar in the small bowl of an electric mixer until light, thick and pale.

add eggs one at a time, beating well between each addition.

add buttermilk.

fold dry ingredients into creamed mixture using a low speed. Scrape down sides of bowl.

spoon into muffin tray.

bake for 20-25 minutes. Test with a skewer which should come out clean.

place 4 choc bits on top of each muffin as soon as you remove them from the oven.

cool slightly before removing from muffin tray to a wire rack.

shared secrets
Decorate muffins with a dollop of cream and grated chocolate for a special treat.

These muffins freeze well.

Freshen muffins in a microwave on Medium for 10-15 seconds per muffin.

muffins - citrus coconut

Makes 16 large or 18 smaller muffins

Grease muffin trays or insert paper patty pans into muffin holes.

preheat oven to 190°C

1 cup gluten free self raising flour

½ cup maize cornflour

½ cup fine polenta

2 teaspoons gluten free baking powder

½ teaspoon bicarbonate of soda

½ cup shredded coconut

125g unsalted butter

¾ cup caster sugar

3 eggs (59g)

2 lemons or limes (or use a combination of both), zest finely grated

⅓ cup lemon or lime juice

½ cup Greek style yogurt

additional ingredients

shredded coconut

sift flours, polenta, baking powder and bicarbonate of soda together.

stir in coconut. Set aside.

cream butter and sugar in the small bowl of an electric mixer until pale and thick.

add eggs one at a time, beating well between each addition. Scrape down sides of bowl.

add grated zest, juice and yogurt.

fold in combined dry ingredients gently, using a low speed or a large metal spoon.

spoon into muffin tray and top with additional shredded coconut.

bake for 20 minutes or until done. Cook only one tray at a time if you do not have a fan-forced oven. Test with a skewer which should come out clean.

cool slightly before removing from muffin tray to a wire rack.

shared secrets

These muffins freeze well.

Freshen muffins in a microwave on Medium for 10-15 seconds per muffin.

'fail-proof' choux pastry

People seem to squirm when it comes to making pastry, especially choux pastry. But it really is so easy and versatile too. What could be more delicious than a delicate éclair or profiterole filled with custard and berries or cream-filled and coated with chocolate or coffee glaze? I do not add sugar to choux pastry as the filling is generally sweet enough. This choux is suitable for savoury fillings too.

Makes approximately 10 large puffs or 18 x 5cm éclairs

Line an oven tray with baking paper.

preheat oven to 220°C

¼ cup gluten free plain flour

¼ cup white rice flour

½ cup water

55g unsalted butter, cut into small cubes

2 eggs (59g)

additional ingredients

1 egg yolk, lightly beaten with 1 tablespoon water to glaze choux (optional)

shared secrets

Baked choux pastries keep well.

Reheat choux in the oven to crisp, if necessary.

Unfilled choux puffs or éclairs freeze very well and will keep for up to 2 months.

When piping choux pastry, stand a knife in a jug filled with hot water and use it to separate the dough from the nozzle. Wipe blade clean after piping each puff/éclair then re-dip knife in hot water again before continuing.

sift flours together, **twice**.

place water and butter into a small saucepan and heat on high until butter has melted. As soon as the water boils add flour all at once.

remove saucepan from heat and beat briefly but vigorously with a wooden spoon until smooth. It will look a bit gluey.

return saucepan to a very low heat for a few seconds and continue to beat until the paste comes cleanly away from sides of saucepan.

transfer choux paste to the small bowl of an electric mixer or food processor.

beat on low speed for 20 seconds.

add eggs one at a time on low speed, beating well between each addition.

increase speed to medium and beat until dough becomes smooth and shiny.

pipe or spoon walnut-sized blobs or éclairs onto prepared oven tray.

glaze tops of choux (optional).

bake for about 20-25 minutes until puffs have risen and are crisp and golden brown.

petite meringues

These dainty little morsels are perfect for afternoon tea.

Makes 25

Line a flat oven tray with baking paper.

preheat oven to 120°C

2 eggs (59g), whites only
pinch of cream of tartar
½ cup caster sugar
vanilla essence

beat egg whites and cream of tartar on high speed until soft peaks form.

add half the sugar (¼ cup) and beat until dissolved. This will take about 3 minutes.

add remaining sugar 1 tablespoon at a time, beating well between additions. If sugar is not dissolved well, droplets of syrup will form and meringues will be sticky.

fold in a few drops of vanilla essence.

pipe small rounds using a 1.5cm nozzle or place small spoonfuls onto baking paper.

bake for about 40-50 minutes or until crisp and dry. Reduce temperature if meringues are browning rather than drying out.

turn oven off and leave oven door slightly ajar until meringues cool.

serve sandwiched together with whipped or coffee-flavoured cream. Alternatively, dip the top of each meringue into melted chocolate.

variation

citrus scented meringues
add orange, lemon or lime zest to the meringue mixture.

shared secrets

Meringues will keep for several days stored in an airtight container.

Serve meringues with beautiful berries for a simple but special dessert.

For pretty pink meringues, stir a drop or two of pink food colouring into the mixture.

raspberry and almond friands

These little cakes are absolutely lovely served with coffee or tea. They are also delicious served as a dessert (see **shared secrets** below).

Makes 8

Lightly grease friand tray.

preheat oven to 200°C

½ cup pure icing sugar

½ cup gluten free plain flour

4 tablespoons finely ground almonds

4 tablespoons shredded coconut

6 tablespoons gluten free breadcrumbs, lightly dried in the oven

100g unsalted butter

4 eggs (59g), whites only

additional ingredients

3 raspberries per friand to garnish

sift icing sugar and flour together.

add almonds, coconut and breadcrumbs then stir to combine.

melt butter in a micro-safe container on Medium for 1 minute or longer if butter is not at room temperature. Set aside.

beat egg whites until firm but not dry.

fold beaten egg whites into almond mixture.

stir butter in lightly.

spoon mixture into friand tray.

place 3 raspberries in the centre of each friand.

bake for about 20-25 minutes or until golden and firm to touch.

test with a skewer which should come out clean.

cool slightly before removing from tray to a wire rack.

shared secrets

Substitute raspberries with blueberries or pitted dark cherries (halve if large).

Add orange or grapefruit zest to friand mixture and top with segments of fruit.

These friands freeze very well.

Freshen friands in a microwave on Medium for 10-15 seconds per friand.

Bake friand mixture in paper or foil-lined patty pans if you do not have a friand tray.

Bake friand mixture in greased timbale moulds if serving as a dessert. Prepare **raspberry sauce** (page 41) and serve with cream.

savoiardi (sponge fingers)

These light sponge fingers are so versatile. They are great with coffee, served with mousse or fruit desserts and of course used in that wonderful Italian dessert, **tiramisu** (page 95).

Makes approximately 24

Line two flat trays with baking paper.

preheat oven to 180°C

3 eggs (59g), separated
¼ cup gluten free plain flour
¼ cup maize cornflour
⅓ cup caster sugar
vanilla essence

additional ingredients

extra caster sugar

place egg whites into the small bowl of an electric mixer.

place yolks into a small dish and whisk with a fork. Set aside.

sift flours together.

whisk egg whites on high speed until soft peaks form.

add sugar gradually, beating until sugar dissolves and mixture becomes shiny.

fold yolks and flour alternately into whites, using a low speed setting. Scrape down the sides of bowl.

stir in a few drops of vanilla essence.

stand a piping bag fitted with a 1.5cm nozzle in a jug. This will catch any mixture that flows from the nozzle.

spoon about half of the sponge mixture into the bag.

pipe 8cm long fingers onto prepared baking trays, leaving room for spreading.

refill piping bag when necessary.

sprinkle tops of savoiardi with extra caster sugar.

bake for about 20-25 minutes or a little longer if you prefer a drier biscuit.

bake one tray at a time, placing second tray into the fridge while the first is cooking. By doing this the egg whites retain their volume.

cool on a wire rack and then store in an airtight container.

shared secret

Sponge fingers will keep well for 2 weeks stored in airtight container.

triple chocolate brownies

It's a winner! My excuse (if I needed one) for creating this treat was being invited to Easter brunch and wanting to take something other than chocolate Easter eggs.

Makes approximately 16 squares

Grease an 18cm square tin and line base with baking paper.

preheat oven to 180°C

for the ganache
¼ cup (50g) dark choc bits
¼ cup cream

for the brownies
100g unsalted butter, roughly chopped
½ cup (100g) dark choc bits
2 eggs (59g)
½ cup brown sugar
¼ cup caster sugar
½ cup Greek style yogurt
2 tablespoons runny honey
¼ cup white rice flour
2 tablespoons maize cornflour
1 tablespoon potato flour
4 tablespoons Dutch style cocoa
½ cup chopped almonds or other nuts
¼ cup (50g) white choc bits

shared secrets
Ganache can be prepared while brownies are baking.

Store brownies in an airtight container in the refrigerator.

The brownies keep well for a week.

The brownies may be frozen.

To cut brownies use a knife that has been dipped into hot water. Dip and wipe blade after each cut.

for the ganache
combine chocolate and cream in a micro-safe container and microwave on Medium for 1 minute, or a little longer if chocolate is not melted. Stir well and set aside.

for the brownies
place butter and chocolate into a micro-safe container and microwave on Medium for 90 seconds or until melted. Stir, then cool slightly.

beat eggs and sugars together in the small bowl of an electric mixer until light and creamy.

add combined melted chocolate and butter, yogurt and honey, beating well.

sift flours and cocoa together and fold into combined mixture.

stir in chopped almonds and white choc bits.

spread into prepared tin.

bake for about 25 minutes. Do not over-bake brownies as they are best a little underdone.

cool in tin for 5 minutes before turning out onto a wire rack.

cool completely before spreading with ganache and leave for an hour to allow ganache to set before cutting (see **shared secrets** before cutting brownies).

serve cut into 4.5cm squares.

chocolate rum and raisin fingers

This slice is quick and easy. It is a real treat for afternoon tea or any time you feel like a fruity chocolate fix.

Makes 28 fingers, measuring 5cm x 3cm

Grease a shallow 22cm square tin and line base with baking paper.

preheat oven to 180°C

½ cup seedless raisins

2 tablespoons dark rum

¼ cup fine polenta

¼ cup maize cornflour

2 tablespoons Dutch style cocoa

⅓ cup caster sugar

½ cup (100g) dark choc bits

¼ cup vegetable oil

2 eggs (59g), separated

combine raisins and rum in a small bowl, allow to stand for 30 minutes.

sift polenta, cornflour and cocoa into a large bowl. Set aside.

combine sugar, chocolate and oil in a micro-safe bowl and microwave on Medium for 2 minutes, stir well and allow to cool a little.

stir egg yolks into cooled chocolate mixture.

add marinated raisins.

whip egg whites until soft peaks form. Using a metal spoon, stir 2 or 3 tablespoons of whites into chocolate mixture. This is to slacken it a little. Fold in remaining whites.

fold sifted mixture into combined chocolate mixture.

spoon into prepared tin.

bake for about 20-25 minutes. Test with a skewer which should come out clean.

serve cut into fingers.

shared secret
This recipe freezes well.

quick sauces & curds

raspberry or strawberry sauce

Frozen raspberries work well and do not need to be rinsed under water.

Makes approximately 1 cup

350g fresh ripe strawberries or raspberries
¼ cup pure icing sugar
2 teaspoons strained lemon juice

rinse and hull fresh berries.

place berries, icing sugar and lemon juice in a food processor and blend until smooth.

press puree through a sieve to remove seeds.

discard seeds.

thin sauce with a little water if necessary.

passionfruit sauce

Makes approximately ½ cup

3 large passionfruit, pulp removed
1 orange, (60ml of strained juice)
2 tablespoons caster sugar
1 teaspoon arrowroot
2 teaspoons water

place passionfruit pulp, orange juice and sugar into a small saucepan.

warm gently to dissolve sugar.

strain mixture over a bowl, then remove and discard about half the seeds.

return juice and remaining seeds to saucepan.

mix arrowroot with water and whisk into the juice.

warm gently, continue to whisk for a few seconds until mixture thickens slightly.

pour into a small dish or jar and allow to cool.

apricot sauce

Makes 1 cup

12 large dried apricots
1 tablespoon caster sugar
½ cup water
⅓ cup strained orange juice
1 tablespoon orange liqueur

place all ingredients in a **deep** micro-safe container and cover with plastic wrap. (This is so that the liquid does not boil over.)

microwave on High for 3 minutes, stir. Re-cover with plastic wrap and microwave for another 2 minutes. Remove plastic wrap carefully.

puree in a food processor until smooth.

add a few tablespoons of extra water to thin sauce if necessary.

press puree through a sieve.

chocolate sauce

Makes approximately 1 cup

125g dark choc bits (or chop block chocolate into small pieces)
¼ cup cream
¼ cup whole milk
1 tablespoon unsalted butter
1 teaspoon golden syrup

combine ingredients in a micro-safe container and microwave on Medium for 2 minutes.

blend with a hand-held electric blender or whisk until sauce is smooth.

allow sauce to cool and thicken.

caramel sauce

Makes 1 cup

50g unsalted butter, cubed
½ cup cream
½ cup brown sugar
a drop or two of balsamic vinegar
  (optional)

place butter, cream and sugar in a micro-safe container and microwave on Medium for 90 seconds.

blend with a hand-held electric blender or whisk until sauce is smooth.

stir in balsamic vinegar (optional).

mango sauce

Makes approximately 1 cup

1 small mango, peel and cut flesh from
  the stone
1-2 tablespoons caster sugar (depending
  on sweetness of the mango)
1 orange (60ml of strained juice)

place ingredients into a food processor and blend until smooth.

thin with more orange juice or a little water if necessary.

chocolate glaze for choux pastries or small cakes

Makes ½ cup

40g unsalted butter, cubed
80g dark choc bits

combine ingredients in a small micro-safe container and microwave on Medium for 1 minute.

stir until chocolate has melted.

chocolate ganache

Makes 1 cup

125g dark choc bits (or block chocolate
    roughly chopped)
½ cup cream
1 tablespoon liqueur (optional)

place chocolate and cream in a micro-safe container and microwave on Medium for 2 minutes.

stir to blend.

add liqueur (optional).

allow sauce to cool and thicken slightly before using.

old-fashioned fudge sauce

Makes approximately 1 cup

50g unsalted butter, cubed
1 tablespoon soft brown sugar
1 tablespoon caster sugar
½ teaspoon instant coffee
½ cup (100g) dark choc bits
¼ cup evaporated milk
1 tablespoon cream

place butter in a micro-safe container and microwave on Medium for 1 minute.

stir in brown sugar, caster sugar and coffee.

add chocolate and stir until it begins to melt.

add evaporated milk and stir well.

place in microwave and cook on Medium for 1 minute.

remove from microwave and add cream.

stir well until fudge is thick and glossy or blend in a food processor. Sauce will continue to thicken as it cools.

lemon or lime curd

Makes ¾ cup

50g unsalted butter, cut into small dice
¼ cup caster sugar
2 eggs (59g), yolks only
2 lemons or limes, finely grated zest and
  ⅓ cup strained juice

place ingredients in a small saucepan.

stir continuously over low heat using a wooden spoon until mixture begins to thicken.

do not boil as the yolks will scramble.

cool curd. It will continue to thicken as it cools.

refrigerate until required.

dried apricot curd

Makes 1¼ cups

100g dried apricots
2 tablespoons caster sugar
⅓ cup water
1 quantity of lemon curd (see recipe above)

place apricots, sugar and water in a **deep** micro-safe container, cover with plastic wrap and microwave on High for 3 minutes, stir.

recover with plastic wrap and microwave another 2 minutes.

remove plastic wrap carefully.

blend in a food processor until smooth, add lemon curd and process again.

cool then refrigerate until required.

passionfruit curd

Makes approximately ¾ cup

50g unsalted butter, cut into small dice
⅓ cup caster sugar
1 teaspoon gluten free custard powder
2 eggs (59g)
juice of 1 lemon
pulp of 6-8 passionfruit

place ingredients into a small saucepan.

stir continuously over low heat using a wooden spoon, until mixture thickens.

do not boil as the yolks will scramble.

cool then refrigerate until required.

shared secrets
Curds are very versatile. They can be used in sponge cakes, tarts and crepes with meringues, and on toast or scones.

cakes & tortes

'v' indicates variation

tips on cake making

Refer to notes on **secrets for success - making and baking gluten free** (page 7).

Most gluten free cakes are best eaten on the day of baking. To freshen cake, warm in microwave on Medium for 10-20 seconds per slice.

If cakes are iced they should be eaten on the day they are made, otherwise the icing will melt if freshened in the microwave.

Do not put cakes containing butter in the fridge as they tend to go very firm, dry out and crumble.

Buttermilk is ideal for use in baking gluten free cakes. The high acid content of buttermilk improves the texture of cakes because it tenderises the flour. It is made from skim milk so it is gentle on the stomach and is almost fat free.

A substitute for buttermilk is 1 cup of milk with 1 tablespoon of lemon juice added. Let stand for 5 minutes before using in baking. You can also replace buttermilk with yogurt.

Often gluten free flours require more liquid than wheat flours, but always err on the side of caution, adding a little at a time.

butter cake

This is an excellent basic plain cake.

Grease a 20cm cake tin or springform tin and line base with baking paper.

preheat oven to 180°C

100g unsalted butter

½ cup caster sugar

vanilla essence

2 eggs (59g), lightly beaten

½ cup gluten free self raising flour

¼ cup maize cornflour

⅓ cup white rice flour

1 teaspoon gluten free baking powder

2 tablespoons milk

cream butter, sugar and a few drops of vanilla essence in the small bowl of an electric mixer until pale and thick.

beat in eggs and scrape down sides of bowl.

sift flours and baking powder together.

fold flour mixture into creamed mixture alternately with the milk.

spoon into prepared tin.

bake for 30 minutes or until cooked when a skewer inserted in the centre comes out clean.

cool cake in tin for 5 minutes before turning out onto a wire rack.

variations

1. cinnamon tea cake
Brush the top of cooked cake with 1 tablespoon melted butter, sprinkle with a combined mixture of 2 teaspoons caster sugar and ½ teaspoon cinnamon.

2. apple and marmalade cake
Prepare butter cake and fold in 1 peeled, cored and diced cooking apple (150g). Spoon into prepared tin. Slice another apple very thinly and arrange slices slightly overlapping on top of cake batter. Glaze with 2 or 3 tablespoons warmed marmalade and sprinkle with caster sugar. Bake at 180°C for approximately 45 minutes.

shared secrets
Butter cake is best eaten on the day it is baked.

Butter cake may be frozen.

To freshen cake, microwave on Medium for 10-20 seconds per slice.

This is an excellent cake for when plain cake crumbs are required in a recipe.

Process any leftover cake and store crumbs in the freezer.

carrot and hazelnut cake with lemon frosting

This cake is delicious served at morning or afternoon tea. It makes a good muffin mix too. Ice with lemon frosting (optional).

Grease a 22cm springform tin and line the base with baking paper.

preheat oven to 160°

for the cake

1 cup gluten free self raising flour

¾ cup maize cornflour

1 teaspoon gluten free baking powder

1 teaspoon bicarbonate of soda

1 teaspoon ground nutmeg

1 teaspoon ground cinnamon

1 cup brown sugar, lightly packed

1½ cups (200g) grated carrot

1 cup hazelnut meal (or grind hazelnuts finely in food processor)

½ cup vegetable oil

½ cup Greek style yogurt

1 teaspoon lemon juice

3 eggs (59g)

for the lemon frosting

100g cream cheese, at room temperature

25g butter, at room temperature

1½ cups pure icing sugar, sift if lumpy

1 teaspoon finely grated lemon zest

2 teaspoons lemon juice

additional ingredients

roasted hazelnuts

for the cake

sift flours, baking powder, bicarbonate of soda and spices together in a large bowl.

stir in sugar, grated carrot and hazelnut meal.

combine oil, yogurt, lemon juice and eggs then stir into flour mixture until batter is smooth. Do not over-beat.

spoon mixture into prepared tin.

bake for about 1 hour or until cooked when a skewer inserted into the centre comes out clean.

cool cake in tin for 5 minutes before turning out onto a wire rack.

ice when cake is cool and garnish with hazelnuts.

for the lemon frosting

combine all ingredients in a food processor or use an electric mixer and beat/blend well.

chocolate hazelnut torte with divine coffee sauce

This is a flat, rich torte that is quick, easy and very delicious. It contains no flour. Double the recipe for a higher torte and bake in a 22cm springform tin.

Serves 6

Grease a 20cm springform tin and line base with baking paper.

preheat oven to 170°C

for the torte

1 teaspoon instant coffee

1 tablespoon cream

⅓ cup caster sugar

½ cup (100g) dark choc bits

50g unsalted butter, cubed

3 eggs (59g), separated

½ cup ground roasted hazelnuts, firmly packed

1 tablespoon Dutch style cocoa

additional ingredients

Dutch style cocoa or pure icing sugar

mascarpone

roasted hazelnuts, chopped to serve with torte (optional)

for the divine coffee sauce

2 tablespoons caster sugar (or to taste)

3 teaspoons instant coffee

2 tablespoons near-boiling water

½ cup cream

for the torte

mix coffee, cream, sugar, choc bits and butter together in a micro-safe container and microwave on Medium for 1 minute, stir. Repeat again. Cool a little.

blend egg yolks and ground hazelnuts into chocolate mixture.

whip egg whites in the small bowl of an electric mixer until soft peaks form.

sift cocoa over whipped whites and fold in to combine.

fold lightly into chocolate mixture, about a third at a time.

spoon into prepared tin.

bake for about 25-30 minutes until cooked when a skewer inserted into the centre comes out clean.

cool in tin for 5 minutes. Place a piece of baking paper onto a wire rack before turning the torte out. Serve upside down as the surface will be smoother.

serve torte dusted with cocoa or icing sugar, **divine coffee sauce**, mascarpone and hazelnuts.

for the divine coffee sauce

dissolve sugar and coffee in the water.

add cream and stir well, or blend in a food processor for a velvety finish.

shared secrets

Boiling water will scald coffee and make it bitter so let water come off the boil before pouring it onto coffee.

Sauce is best prepared on the day. Torte can be made in advance and will keep for several days.

Torte may be frozen.

chocolate orange torte with boozy star anise oranges

Seriously fabulous and amazingly light! This torte contains no butter.

Serves 8-10

Grease a 24cm springform tin and line base and sides with baking paper.

preheat oven to 160°C

for the torte

¾ cup whole un-blanched almonds

⅓ cup (70g) dark choc bits

½ cup stale gluten free breadcrumbs or cake crumbs

2 tablespoons Dutch style cocoa

¾ teaspoon gluten free baking powder

4 eggs (59g), separated

¾ cup caster sugar

1 orange, finely grated zest

¼ cup strained orange juice

1 tablespoon orange liqueur

additional ingredients

mascarpone

for the torte

place almonds into a food processor bowl and whizz until they are roughly ground.

add choc bits and process until you have a fairly fine texture.

add breadcrumbs, cocoa and sift in baking powder. Blend to combine.

whisk egg whites in the large bowl of an electric mixer until soft peaks form. Set aside briefly.

beat yolks and sugar until thick and creamy in the small bowl of an electric mixer.

add orange zest, juice and liqueur and beat lightly together.

fold this mixture into beaten whites.

stir in crumbly chocolate mixture.

pour into prepared tin.

bake for about 50 minutes or until cooked when a skewer inserted into the centre comes out clean.

place tin on a wire rack, leave for 5 minutes before releasing torte from tin.

place a piece of baking paper onto a wire rack and invert torte onto it.

cool completely before removing baking paper from base and sides of torte.

cut torte upside down and serve with **boozy star anise oranges**, syrup and mascarpone.

continued on next page

chocolate orange torte with boozy star anise oranges *(continued)*

for the boozy star anise oranges

3-4 large oranges, allow 6 segments per serve (see first instruction)

plus 2 large oranges

1 large lemon, strained juice only (you will need ¾ cup of combined lemon and orange juice)

½ cup sugar

3 tablespoons orange liqueur

1 star anise

for the boozy star anise oranges

prepare first oranges listed, peeling as close to the flesh as you can. Remove any white membrane and then slice between the segments. Remove any seeds.

place segments into a bowl and set aside until you are ready to plate the torte.

using a vegetable peeler or knife, cut rind from the remaining two oranges into long strips. Remove white pith or else the syrup will be bitter. Slice orange strips very finely.

squeeze juice from the two oranges and combine it with the lemon juice.

strain combined juice into a small saucepan.

add rind, sugar, liqueur and star anise.

boil for 10 minutes to reduce to a syrupy consistency.

pour syrup over reserved orange segments when you plate the torte.

shared secrets

This torte keeps well for several days.

Torte may be warmed in a microwave on Medium for 10-20 seconds per slice.

Torte may be frozen.

Syrup may be made up to a week in advance.

Prepare orange segments on the day.

carrot, pecan and polenta cake

This simple, yummy cake is thrown together, stirred and baked with a minimum of fuss. Great with a cuppa anytime.

Grease a 20cm or 22cm springform tin and line base with baking paper.

preheat oven to 160°C

1 cup gluten free self raising flour

¼ cup maize cornflour

½ cup fine polenta

½ teaspoon bicarbonate of soda

1 teaspoon ground cinnamon

1 cup soft brown sugar, lightly packed

2 cups (250g) grated carrot

3 eggs (59g)

125g unsalted butter, melted

additional ingredients

½ cup pecan nuts to decorate top of cake

sift flours, polenta, bicarbonate of soda and cinnamon together.

stir in sugar, breaking up any lumps.

add grated carrot and stir again.

place eggs into a small bowl and whisk with a fork.

stir eggs and melted butter into flour mixture.

pour into prepared cake tin and decorate top with pecan nuts.

bake for about 40-50 minutes or until cooked when a skewer inserted into the centre comes out clean.

cool in tin for 5 minutes before turning out onto a wire rack.

gingerbread cake

Gingerbread is compatible with ginger, sultanas, raisins, currants and nuts, so feel free to vary this basic recipe.

Grease a deep 22cm square tin and line base with baking paper.

preheat oven to 160°C

½ cup golden syrup

½ cup milk

1 teaspoon bicarbonate of soda

100g soft unsalted butter

½ cup brown sugar, firmly packed

2 eggs (59g)

1½ cups gluten free plain flour

1 teaspoon ground ginger

½ teaspoon ground cinnamon

½ teaspoon ground nutmeg

pinch of ground cloves

additional ingredients (optional)
lemon butter icing *(page 57)*

place golden syrup and milk in a micro-safe container and microwave on Medium for 2 minutes. Stir in bicarbonate of soda and set aside.

cream butter and sugar in the small bowl of an electric mixer until pale and thick.

beat in the eggs. Scrape down sides of bowl.

sift flour and spices together.

beat in some flour mixture, then some of the liquid, alternating until batter is smooth.

pour into prepared tin.

bake for about 45 minutes or until cooked when a skewer inserted into the centre comes out clean.

cool cake in tin for 5 minutes before turning out onto a rack.

ice with **lemon butter icing**.

lemon buttermilk cake

Serves 8

Grease a 22cm round cake tin and line base with baking paper.

preheat oven to 180°C

for the cake

1 cup gluten free self raising flour

½ cup maize cornflour

1 teaspoon gluten free baking powder

125g unsalted butter

¾ cup caster sugar

1 tablespoon finely grated lemon zest

2 eggs (59g), separated

½ cup buttermilk or Greek style yogurt

¼ cup strained lemon juice

for the lemon butter icing

1 cup pure icing sugar

30g soft unsalted butter

*1 lemon, finely grated zest and
   1 tablespoon strained juice*

for the cake

sift flours and baking powder together. Set aside.

cream butter, sugar and lemon zest in the small bowl of an electric mixer until pale and thick.

add yolks, buttermilk and lemon juice. It will curdle but ignore this.

fold in sifted mixture using a low speed. Transfer batter to a large mixing bowl.

whip egg whites in a clean small bowl of an electric mixer until soft peaks form.

fold into batter about a third at a time, using a large metal spoon.

pour or spoon into prepared tin.

bake for about 50 minutes or until cooked when a skewer inserted into the centre comes out clean.

cool cake in the tin for 5 minutes before turning out onto a wire rack.

ice cake when completely cool.

for the lemon butter icing

combine all ingredients in a food processor and blend until smooth.

lemon coconut cake

This is a scrumptious cake with the zing of lemon.

Grease an 18cm cake tin and line base with baking paper.

This recipe may be doubled and baked in a 30cm x 20cm cake tin.

preheat oven to 180°C

for the cake

½ cup gluten free self raising flour

½ cup fine polenta

1 teaspoon gluten free baking powder

¼ cup shredded coconut

¼ cup blanched almond meal

125g unsalted butter

¾ cup caster sugar

1 tablespoon finely grated lemon zest

2 eggs (59g), separated

½ cup sour cream

⅓ cup strained lemon juice

for the glaze

2 tablespoons caster sugar

1 lemon, strained juice only

for the cake

sift flour, polenta and baking powder together.

stir in coconut and almond meal. Set aside.

cream butter, sugar and lemon zest in the small bowl of an electric mixer until pale and thick.

add egg yolks, sour cream and lemon juice, beating well. Transfer mixture to a larger bowl.

whip egg whites in a clean small bowl of an electric mixer until soft peaks form.

fold whites into creamed mixture and then lightly fold in dry ingredients.

pour or spoon into prepared tin

bake for about 35-40 minutes or until cooked when a skewer inserted into the centre comes out clean.

prepare glaze and brush over cake as soon as it is removed from oven.

cool in tin for 5 minutes before turning out onto a wire rack.

for the glaze

combine the sugar and juice.

stir until sugar dissolves.

moist apple and walnut crumble cake

This is a luscious afternoon teacake.

Grease an 11cm x 21cm loaf tin or 20cm springform tin and line base with baking paper.

preheat oven to 180°C

for the crumble

¾ cup roughly chopped walnuts

2 tablespoons brown sugar

½ teaspoon ground cinnamon

for the cake

1 cooking apple (approximately 170g)

125g unsalted butter

⅓ cup caster sugar

2 eggs (59g)

¾ cup gluten free self raising flour

¼ cup buckwheat flour

¼ cup maize cornflour

½ teaspoon ground cinnamon

1 teaspoon gluten free baking powder

½ cup milk (approximately)

1 tablespoon brandy (optional)

for the crumble

process crumble ingredients and set aside.

for the cake

peel, core and grate apple. Set aside briefly.

cream butter and sugar in the small bowl of an electric mixer until pale and thick.

add eggs one at a time. Scrape down sides of bowl.

sift flours, cinnamon and baking powder together.

add to creamed mixture with about ¼ cup milk. Do not over-beat.

fold in apple and brandy gently.

add remainder of milk only if batter is too stiff.

spoon about half the batter into prepared tin, sprinkle with half the crumble.

spoon in remaining batter and sprinkle with remainder of crumble.

bake for about 30-40 minutes or until cooked when a skewer inserted into the centre comes out clean.

cool in tin for 5 minutes before turning out onto a wire rack.

moist orange and polenta cake with citrus drizzle

Serves 6

Grease a 22cm round cake tin and line base with baking paper.

preheat oven to 180°C

for the cake

2 oranges (approximately 200g each) **do not peel**

¾ cup sugar

¾ cup boiling water

1 tablespoon orange liqueur

¼ cup fine polenta

¼ cup white rice flour

½ cup ground almonds, not too finely ground as we want a bit of texture

125g unsalted butter

½ cup caster sugar

2 eggs (59g)

additional ingredients

cream to serve

for the drizzle

1 orange and 1 lemon, rind and strained juice

1 teaspoon runny honey

3 tablespoons sugar

1 tablespoon orange liqueur

shared secrets

Orange and polenta cake and drizzle will keep well for 3 days.

Cake and drizzle may be reheated in a microwave on Medium.

Cake may be frozen.

for the cake

cut oranges in half, remove pips and roughly chop.

puree unpeeled oranges in a food processor (they will look coarse).

transfer pureed oranges to a small saucepan.

add ¾ cup sugar, boiling water and liqueur.

boil mixture for 15-20 minutes, stirring occasionally until the liquid has all but evaporated.

remove from heat and allow to cool slightly.

sift polenta and rice flour together.

stir in ground almonds and set aside.

cream butter and sugar in the small bowl of an electric mixer until pale and thick.

add eggs one at a time, beating well.

stir in sifted mixture and then the puree.

spoon into prepared tin.

bake for 35-40 minutes or until cooked when a skewer inserted into the centre comes out clean.

cool in tin for 5 minutes before turning out onto a wire rack.

serve cake cut in wedges with **drizzle** and softly whipped cream.

for the drizzle

using a vegetable peeler or knife, cut rind from fruit in long strips. Remove white pith and slice very finely.

place all of the ingredients for the drizzle into a small saucepan.

boil rapidly to reduce a little.

remove from heat to cool.

sponge cake

Grease a 20cm sandwich tin with melted butter and line base with baking paper.

Mix 1 teaspoon each of maize cornflour and caster sugar, then using a tea strainer sift mixture to dust insides of the tin, turning it around as you dust. The sponge needs to cling to sides of the tin enabling it to rise.

preheat oven to 190°C

2 eggs (59g)

⅓ cup caster sugar

¼ cup maize cornflour

1 tablespoon gluten free self raising flour

¼ cup gluten free custard powder

½ teaspoon cream of tartar

¼ teaspoon bicarbonate of soda

1 tablespoon unsalted butter, melted

1 tablespoon boiling water

shared secrets

Adding boiling water to the sponge starts the cooking process.

Sponge may be prepared in advance and will remain fresh for 2 days.

Sponge may be frozen and will keep for up to 3 months.

Stale sponge can be used in **tiramisu** (page 95), fruit trifles and tortes.

Jelly cakes freeze very well.

boil kettle while assembling ingredients, so that the water is ready to use in the recipe.

beat eggs and sugar in the small bowl of an electric mixer, on the highest speed setting for 5 minutes until thick and creamy.

sift flours, custard powder, cream of tartar and bicarbonate of soda together.

fold sifted mixture very gently through egg mixture using the lowest speed setting until just combined.

add melted butter and boiling water. Do not over-beat.

spoon into prepared tin.

bake for about 20 minutes or until sponge springs back when pressed lightly in the centre.

cool sponge in tin for about 5 minutes before turning out onto a wire rack. Leave baking paper on the sponge base until it is cool as this will stop the sponge from shrinking.

variation
sweet old-fashioned jelly cakes

Prepare sponge cake batter and bake in greased mini muffin tins. Prepare gluten free flavoured jellies (for each jelly you will require 60g jelly crystals to 375g boiling water). Partially set in refrigerator. Jelly should be sloppy. Dip cakes into jelly, then roll in coconut. Refrigerate and when the jelly is set, cut each cake on a slant and pipe with whipped cream.

sponge cake with caramelised nectarines

This is a very simple and delicious dessert. It is equally fabulous with caramelised apples or pears, syrupy plums, peaches or rhubarb.

Serves 4-6

sponge cake (page 63)

for the caramelised nectarines

4 large perfectly ripe freestone nectarines (avoid over-ripe fruit)

½ cup caster sugar

¼ cup water

additional ingredients

cream, mascarpone or custard for serving

prepare and bake sponge cake.

cut sponge in thin slices, wedges, cubes or oval shapes using metal cutters.

for the caramelised nectarines

cut each nectarine into quarters, remove stone.

heat a heavy-based pan over medium heat.

sprinkle sugar over base of pan and add water.

boil until caramel begins to turn golden in colour. Do not stir as it will crystallise.

add fruit and turn over gently as it caramelises. Turn heat down so that the sugar does not scorch. Add a little extra water if caramel is browning too quickly.

remove pan from heat.

serve warm or at room temperature with sponge and a dollop of whipped cream, mascarpone and/or custard.

shared secrets

Sponge may be prepared in advance and frozen.

Nectarines are best prepared close to serving time as they may discolour.

Nectarines may also be sprinkled with caster sugar and grilled.

crepes & hotcakes

'v' indicates variation

crepes 1

I have included two basic crepe recipes and both are excellent. One contains more flour and less eggs, the other less flour and more eggs.

Makes 8 crepes

1 cup gluten free plain flour

2 eggs (59g)

1¼ cups milk (enough to make a thin batter like pouring cream)

1 tablespoon unsalted butter, melted

additional ingredients

unsalted butter for frying

shared secrets

Crepes may be made by hand using a wire whisk, in a food processor or electric mixer.

Crepes may be prepared in advance.

Crepes may be layered with freezer wrap and frozen.

sift flour.

place flour, eggs and milk in a food processor and blend until smooth.

add melted butter and whizz briefly again.

pour batter into a 1 litre capacity jug.

allow batter to rest for 10 minutes before cooking crepes.

heat a crepe pan, brush surface of pan with some extra butter.

pour in enough crepe batter (use a 60ml ladle or alternatively 3 tablespoons) to cover base of pan with a thin coating of batter. Tilt and shake the pan to distribute batter evenly.

cook over medium/high heat until top of crepe sets and edges turn golden brown. Briefly remove pan from heat then turn crepe using a spatula and fingers, and cook other side. (Be careful not to burn the tips of your fingers.)

slide crepe from pan onto a wire rack or plate and cover with foil or a clean tea towel. If you are not using a non-stick pan, wipe pan with a paper towel and grease again with butter. Do this after you have made each crepe.

stir batter between making each crepe.

continue cooking crepes until all mixture is used.

crepes 2

Makes 6-8 crepes

⅓ cup gluten free plain flour

3 eggs (59g)

¾ cup milk

1 tablespoon unsalted butter, melted

additional ingredients
unsalted butter for frying

sift flour.

place flour in a food processor.

whisk eggs and milk together in a jug.

pour onto flour through the feed tube, continuing to process until smooth.

add melted butter and whizz again.

pour batter into a 1 litre capacity jug.

allow batter to rest for 10 minutes before making crepes (see **crepes 1**, previous page).

stir batter between making each crepe.

shared secrets

Crepes may be made by hand using a wire whisk, in a food processor or electric mixer.

Crepes may be prepared in advance.

Crepes may be layered with freezer wrap and frozen.

apple caramel crepes

Serves 6-8

for the crepes
crepes 1 or crepes 2 *(page 66/67)*

for the filling
4-6 large cooking apples
  (approximately 600g)
60g unsalted butter
½ cup soft brown sugar
1 lemon, grated zest and strained juice
¼ teaspoon ground cinnamon
1 tablespoon brandy or Calvados
1-2 tablespoons cream

additional ingredients
pure icing sugar
chopped walnuts (optional)
*cream or **pouring custard** (page 92)*
ice cream, gluten free

for the crepes
prepare crepes.

for the filling
peel core and thinly slice apples.

melt butter and sugar gently in a wide-based frypan.

add zest, juice, cinnamon and apples then simmer, turning apples occasionally.

cook gently until fruit softens and caramelises, but still holds its shape. This will take about 10-15 minutes. The liquid will reduce.

add brandy and cream. Continue cooking until apples are coated with caramel.

to plate the dessert
take one crepe, fold into quarters and place onto a dessert plate. Repeat process with each crepe.

warm apples in a microwave oven or frypan and spoon into the top pocket of each crepe.

dust crepes with icing sugar just before serving.

garnish with a scattering of chopped walnuts.

serve with cream, pouring custard or ice cream.

shared secrets
Crepes may be prepared in advance.

Apple filling is best prepared on the day.

poppy seed crepes with lemon curd and raspberries

Serves 6-8

for the crepes
crepes 1 or crepes 2 *(page 66/67)*
1 teaspoon poppy seeds

for the filling
lemon curd *(page 44), double quantity*

for the raspberries
2 or 3 punnets of fresh raspberries, picked over to remove any stems, rinse and drain well.

caster sugar (to taste)

additional ingredients
pure icing sugar
whipped cream to serve

for the crepes
prepare crepe batter, adding poppy seeds to the mixture.
make as per instructions.

for the filling
prepare curd

for the raspberries
place raspberries in a bowl, sprinkle with sugar and marinate for 10 minutes.

to plate the dessert
take one crepe and spread lemon curd over half of the crepe.

fold over and then in half again.

place crepe on a dessert plate.

repeat above process with each crepe.

spoon raspberries onto each plate. Sprinkle with caster sugar.

dust crepes with icing sugar and serve with whipped cream.

shared secrets
Lemon curd may be lightened with ½ cup whipped cream.

Lemon curd may be made up to 3 days in advance.

Crepes may be made in advance but preferably on the day, for this dessert.

coconut crepe cones with soft yogurt whip and mango sauce

Serves 8

for the crepes

crepes 1 *(page 66)*

8 tablespoons shredded coconut

mango sauce *(page 42)*

for the soft yogurt whip

1½ cups cream

2-3 tablespoons pure icing sugar, sift if it is lumpy

1 cup Greek style yogurt

additional ingredients

4 mangoes, peel and slice each cheek into long thin strips. Allow 5 or 6 slices per crepe.

shared secrets

Coconut crepes are best prepared on the day and assembled close to serving time.

Soft yogurt whip is best prepared close to serving time.

Mango sauce may be prepared a day in advance.

for the crepes

prepare crepe batter. Set aside.

toast shredded coconut lightly.

sprinkle 1 tablespoon of coconut over base of a heated, lightly greased crepe pan and pour in enough batter to cover the base with a thin coating. Cook as per instructions for crepes 1 recipe. Repeat until you have used all the batter.

prepare mango sauce.

for the soft yogurt whip

whip cream and icing sugar until thick.

add yogurt and beat briefly to combine.

refrigerate until required.

to plate the dessert

place crepes onto a work bench.

divide soft yogurt whip between crepes and spread over half of each crepe.

place 5 or 6 mango slices over the soft yogurt whip, extending mango over the edge by 1cm. Repeat for each crepe.

fold unfilled side of crepe over the filled half.

roll crepes into a cone shape by placing your index finger on the centre point of the folded crepe and roll from one corner to the other.

place crepe cones onto dessert plates.

serve with **mango sauce**.

hotcakes with banana, yogurt and honey

My love of banana, honey and yogurt stems from a visit to the Greek Islands. Use Greek style yogurt for this recipe.

Makes approximately 20 hotcakes

I like to use a 15cm crepe pan for hotcakes but any shallow frypan will suffice.

for the hotcakes
½ cup gluten free self raising flour

½ cup white rice flour

½ teaspoon gluten free baking powder

½ teaspoon bicarbonate of soda

2 eggs (59g)

2 tablespoons caster sugar

⅓ cup milk soured with ½ teaspoon lemon juice

2 tablespoons unsalted butter, melted

additional ingredients
unsalted butter for frying

Greek style yogurt

ripe bananas

runny honey

walnuts (optional)

sift flours, baking powder and bicarbonate of soda together.

beat eggs and sugar together in the small bowl of an electric mixer until thick and creamy.

add soured milk and melted butter.

fold in flour mixture using a low speed.

heat crepe pan and lightly grease with some of the extra butter.

add 2 tablespoons of batter (per hotcake) allowing room for spreading. When bubbles appear and begin to burst, turn hotcake over to brown lightly on other side.

remove to a wire rack, cover with a clean cloth to keep warm.

repeat until all of the mixture is used.

serve hotcakes with a good dollop of yogurt, sliced banana, a drizzle of honey and a scattering of roughly chopped walnuts.

variations
1. blueberry hotcakes
Place 6 or more blueberries onto each hotcake immediately after pouring the batter into pan and cook as above. Serve with mascarpone or cream.

2. hotcakes with oven baked rhubarb (page 107)
Prepare hotcakes and serve with oven baked rhubarb, Greek style yogurt and pistachio nuts.

shared secret
As sweet as a kiss! Hotcakes may be cooked in metal non-stick pancake shapes - a good example of this is the heart shape that can be used on Valentine's Day!

layered apple crepe cake

This elegant layered 'cake' tastes and looks very impressive.

Serves 8

Line a flat oven tray with baking paper.

preheat oven to 170°C

for the crepes
crepes 1 or crepes 2 *(page 66/67)*

for the filling
14 large cooking apples
1 lemon, juice only
75g unsalted butter
1 cup caster sugar (or to taste depending on the sweetness of the apples)
1 teaspoon ground cinnamon
½ teaspoon ground nutmeg
1-2 tablespoons brandy (optional)

additional ingredients
caramel sauce *(page 42)*
cream to serve

shared secrets

For a higher cake, cook extra crepes and apples.

Apples may be prepared several days in advance.

The cake may be prepared several days in advance.

The assembled cake may also be frozen.

The cake may be reheated in the oven or microwave oven.

Crepe alternative - substitute chestnut flour for gluten free plain flour.

for the crepes
prepare crepes. Set aside.

for the filling
prepare apples by peeling and coring. Place apples in a bowl of water containing lemon juice. This will prevent discolouration.

cut apples in thin even slices.

cook apples in batches according to the size of your frypan.

place some butter, sugar and spices in the pan.

add some of the apples and cook on medium/high heat for about 10 minutes until tender but still holding their shape. Turn occasionally.

add some brandy if using and increase heat to reduce liquid.

remove apples from pan to a bowl. Set aside.

repeat until all apples are cooked.

to assemble the cake

place one crepe on prepared oven tray.

cover crepe with a thin layer of apples. Do this by placing apple slices around the edge of crepe and then fill in remaining surface of the crepe with a thin layer of apples.

continue layering crepes and apples until you have eight layers to your cake.

cover loosely with foil and refrigerate. (Remove from fridge 1-2 hours before baking).

bake covered cake for 30-45 minutes or until warm.

to serve the cake

cut into wedges with an electric knife or a sharp thin-bladed knife. Use a cake lifter to place a wedge onto each dessert plate.

serve with **caramel sauce** and softly whipped cream.

crepes with banana and old-fashioned fudge sauce

I find that one crepe per person is sufficient, as the fudge sauce is deliciously rich.

Serves 6

crepes 2 *(page 67)*

old-fashioned fudge sauce *(page 42)*

3 perfectly ripe bananas

vanilla ice cream, gluten free

*¼ cup roasted hazelnuts (see **shared secrets**)*

additional ingredients
pure icing sugar (optional)

prepare crepes. Set aside.

prepare old-fashioned fudge sauce.

to plate the crepes

peel and slice bananas on an angle.

take one crepe, fold into quarters and place on a dessert plate.

lift the top pocket and slide in half of one sliced banana.

spoon in a tablespoon of fudge sauce, letting some spill over onto the plate. If sauce has been refrigerated, thin it in the microwave on Medium for 20-30 seconds.

repeat until you have prepared all of the crepes.

place a scoop of ice cream on plates, drizzle with a little more sauce and top with hazelnuts.

dust crepes with icing sugar.

shared secrets

Crepes may be made in advance, but are best prepared on the day.

Old-fashioned fudge sauce may be prepared up to 5 days in advance.

Dessert best assembled just before serving.

To roast hazelnuts, place them on an oven tray and roast at 180°C for about 10-15 minutes until skins darken. Remove from oven and place in a clean towel. Rub vigorously to remove skins.

crumbles 'n crunch

baked peaches with amaretti crumble

Choose freestone peaches that are ripe but not over-ripe. If peaches are large, allow half per person, if small allow 2 halves per person.

Serves 6

Generously grease a shallow ovenproof dish that is large enough to hold the fruit.

preheat oven to 180°C

for the fruit

3 large or 6 smaller peaches

½ cup strained orange juice

for the crumble

*½ cup **amaretti biscuit** crumbs
(page 15)*

½ cup chopped blanched almonds

*1 tablespoon light brown sugar or
caster sugar*

1 orange, zest finely grated

2 tablespoons unsalted butter

additional ingredients

*ice cream, gluten free and/or cream to
serve*

for the fruit

halve peaches, remove stones and place in dish.

drizzle orange juice around peaches but not in peach cavity.

for the crumble

mix crumbs, almonds, sugar, zest and butter together using your fingers, working butter through until you have a crumbly mixture.

fill each peach cavity with crumble.

bake for 20-30 minutes or until cooked but not too soft, and crumble is golden.

serve peaches with ice cream or cream and a drizzle of orange syrup from the dish.

shared secrets

Substitute nectarines for peaches.

Crumble may be prepared several days in advance and stored in refrigerator.

Peaches and nectarines are best baked just prior to eating.

To crumble amaretti biscuits, place in a freezer bag and crush with a rolling pin.

peaches with hazelnut crunch

Serves 6

Grease six individual ovenproof dishes or one large dish.

preheat oven to 180°C

for the fruit

6 large firm ripe freestone peaches

for the crunch

*1 cup stale gluten free cake crumbs (**butter cake** page 47 or **sponge cake** recipe page 63)*

¼ cup skinned hazelnuts, finely chopped

2 tablespoons caster sugar

2 tablespoons unsalted butter

2 tablespoons Frangelico (hazelnut liqueur)

additional ingredients

vanilla ice cream, gluten free or whipped cream to serve

for the fruit

blanch peaches in boiling water for 1-2 minutes to remove skins.

cut peaches in halves, then into thick slices and divide between dish/es.

for the crunch

mix cake crumbs, nuts, sugar and butter together, working butter in with your fingers.

scatter crunch evenly over fruit.

drizzle with liqueur.

bake for about 20 minutes or until peaches are soft and crunch is lightly browned.

serve with vanilla ice cream or whipped cream.

shared secrets

Crunch may be made several days in advance and stored in refrigerator.

Peaches best baked just prior to eating.

apple, pear and pecan crumble

Serves 4

Grease 4 x 175ml ovenproof dishes.

preheat oven to 180°C

for the fruit

2 large cooking apples

2 large cooking pears

1 lemon, zest finely grated

2 teaspoons lemon juice

*2 tablespoons brown or caster sugar
(add more sugar if the apples are tart)*

¼ teaspoon ground nutmeg

¼ teaspoon ground cinnamon

1 tablespoon unsalted butter

for the crumble

2 tablespoons gluten free plain flour

2 tablespoons brown sugar

¾ cup chopped pecan nuts

⅓ cup coconut

2 tablespoons soft unsalted butter

additional ingredients

cheat's custard *(page 85)*

cream to serve

for the fruit

peel and core apples and pears. Cut fruit into 2cm pieces.

mix apples, pears, zest, juice, sugar and spices together.

melt butter in a shallow frypan.

add combined fruit and cook on medium heat for about 5 minutes, gently turning fruit occasionally. The fruit should be just cooked, not mushy.

spoon into prepared dishes.

for the crumble

combine crumble ingredients, working butter through with your fingers.

sprinkle crumble over fruit.

bake for 20-30 minutes or until crumble turns golden brown.

serve with **cheat's custard** and cream if desired.

nectarine and blueberry crunch

The soft fruit and crunchy texture of the topping makes this a great combination.

Serve in individual ovenproof dishes, or alternatively make one larger dish if you wish. The number of desserts the recipe makes depends on the size of the nectarines.

Serves 4-6

Grease four to six individual ovenproof dishes.

preheat oven to 180°C

for the fruit

4-6 large nectarines

1 punnet (150g) fresh or frozen blueberries

1 orange, strained juice only

1 tablespoon caster sugar

for the crunch

2 tablespoons chopped nuts (blanched almonds or raw cashew nuts)

2 tablespoons shredded coconut

*2 tablespoons **amaretti biscuit** crumbs (page 15)*

2 tablespoons gluten free bread crumbs

2 tablespoons white rice flour

2 tablespoons caster sugar

2 tablespoons unsalted butter

additional ingredients

whipped cream to serve

for the fruit

halve nectarines, remove stones and cut into wedges.

mix nectarines and blueberries gently together in a large bowl.

pour orange juice over and sprinkle with sugar.

divide mixture between ovenproof dishes.

for the crunch

place crunch ingredients into a bowl and work butter through with your fingers.

sprinkle crunch over fruit.

bake for 20-25 minutes or until golden.

serve warm or hot straight from the oven with whipped cream.

shared secrets

Substitute peaches for nectarines.

Crunch may be prepared up to a week in advance and stored in refrigerator.

Nectarines and peaches are best prepared just prior to baking.

custard desserts

'v' indicates variation

cheat's custard

This versatile custard can be used in choux pastries, crepes, tarts and tartlet cases.

Makes 1¼ cups

2 eggs (59g), yolks only

1 tablespoon maize cornflour

1 tablespoon gluten free custard powder

2 tablespoons caster sugar (or to taste)

1 cup milk

1 teaspoon unsalted butter

1 tablespoon cream

vanilla essence

additional ingredients

*½ cup cream (optional - see **shared secrets**)*

place egg yolks, cornflour, custard powder and sugar into a small saucepan and stir to combine.

whisk in milk gradually until well blended.

simmer gently on medium/low heat, whisking constantly until custard begins to thicken.

remove from heat as soon as custard thickens. **Do not boil** as the egg will scramble.

add butter, cream and a few drops of vanilla essence to taste.

press plastic wrap gently over surface of custard to prevent a skin forming.

shared secrets

For liqueur custard add a tablespoon of Grand Marnier or Cointreau.

For coffee-flavoured custard, add 2 teaspoons (or to taste) instant coffee dissolved in a little hot water when you add the milk.

Custard may be prepared in advance and will keep well refrigerated for several days.

To lighten the cooled custard, fold through ½ cup whipped cream.

If custard becomes too thick or lumpy, whizz it in a food processor until smooth.

To thin custard add more milk or cream and whisk well.

Freeze egg whites for later use.

honey panna cotta

I think this is one of the sexiest desserts ever! You will not believe how easy it is to prepare. Panna cotta teams well with mixed berries, fresh raspberries, grilled mangoes, baked plums, rosy-red quinces, pears or passionfruit.

Serves 6

Prepare 6 x 125ml dariole or timbale moulds by brushing with grapeseed or almond oil.

3 teaspoons gelatine

2 tablespoons warm water

1 cup milk

3 tablespoons honey or to taste

1 cup cream

vanilla essence

shared secrets

For a lower fat/sugar panna cotta use a combination of skim milk, cream and yogurt. Reduce the honey by half.

To prepare 4 larger serves of panna cotta, fill moulds to the brim or use 150ml moulds.

May be prepared one day in advance.

When measuring honey, lightly oil a measuring spoon or cup as this will allow the liquid to slip free easily.

Remove panna cotta from refrigerator about 30 minutes before serving.

sprinkle gelatine over warm water and microwave on Medium for 30-40 seconds or until dissolved, stir well.

heat milk with honey in a micro-safe container on High for 2 minutes, stir until honey melts.

strain dissolved gelatine into the hot liquid immediately, stir well.

whisk in cream and a few drops of vanilla essence to taste.

place moulds on a small flat tray, pour custard into moulds to within 1cm of the rim.

cover loosely with plastic wrap and chill for 3-4 hours.

to serve

remove panna cotta from moulds by running a thin-bladed knife around the edge of the custard. Lightly brush the top of each custard with water. That way, if the dessert is not centred it is easy to slide over. Invert panna cotta onto plates and serve with fruit of your choice.

variation

rum panna cotta with marinated prunes

Replace vanilla with 1-2 teaspoons of Jamaican rum and serve with pitted prunes marinated overnight or preferably longer in orange-flavoured liqueur.

baked honey custard with stewed dried apricots

Lightly grease 1 x 700ml shallow ovenproof dish, 4 x 175ml or 4 x 200ml individual pudding moulds. Cooking time will depend on the depth of container used.

preheat oven to 160°C

for the custard
50ml runny honey (or to taste)
200ml whole milk
200ml cream
3 eggs (59g) + 1 yolk
ground nutmeg to finish

for the apricots
1 cup water
⅓ cup sugar
250g dried apricots

shared secrets
Custard best prepared on the day.

Apricots may be prepared in advance and refrigerated for up to a week.

When measuring honey, lightly oil a measuring spoon or cup as this will allow the liquid to slip free easily.

for the custard

place honey and 100ml of milk in a micro-safe jug and microwave on Medium for 1 minute or until the honey is dissolved.

add remaining milk and cream.

beat in eggs and yolk using a hand-held electric blender or wire whisk.

pour into ovenproof dish/moulds.

dust with nutmeg.

place in a bain-marie (refer **secrets for success making and baking gluten free - bain-marie** page 7).

bake for about 30-35 minutes for one large dish or about 25 minutes for individual dishes or until custard is set.

serve warm or at room temperature with apricots.

for the apricots

place ingredients together in a **deep** micro-safe container.

cover with plastic wrap and microwave on High for 4 minutes, stir. Re-cover with plastic wrap and microwave for another 4 minutes. Carefully remove plastic wrap.

stir then microwave uncovered for another 2 minutes.

chocolate mocha martinis

This lusciously smooth custard (mocha crème patissiere) topped with ganache is so elegant and delicious. For a classy presentation serve this dessert in martini glasses.

Serves 4

Frost rims of 4 x 180ml martini glasses

for the frosting

1 egg (59g), white only

2 tablespoons coffee sugar crystals or demerara sugar

for the chocolate mocha custard

3 teaspoons instant coffee

400ml milk

2 eggs (59g), yolks only

2 tablespoons maize cornflour

1 tablespoon + 2 teaspoons brown sugar firmly packed

½ cup (100g) dark choc bits

1 tablespoon cream

for the ganache

¼ cup (50g) dark choc bits

¼ cup cream

for the frosting

froth egg white lightly with a fork and pour onto a plate.

place sugar crystals into a food processor and whizz until crushed but not too powdery.

transfer crushed crystals to a small plate.

dip each glass rim into egg white then into crushed crystals.

for the chocolate mocha custard

place coffee, milk, yolks, cornflour and sugar into a food processor and blend until smooth.

transfer to a small saucepan and cook over **medium/low** heat, stirring constantly with a whisk or wooden spoon until custard thickens. **Do not** leave stove or custard may spoil.

remove from heat.

add choc bits and cream. Stir to blend.

whizz in a food processor for a velvety finish. Transfer to a jug.

pour custard into glasses, filling to within 5mm of the rim.

smooth top of custards with the back of a spoon. Try to keep surface level.

place glasses on a tray. To prevent a skin forming on the custards, rest a sheet of baking paper lightly on top of the glasses.

refrigerate until custard is set.

for the ganache

place choc bits and cream in a micro-safe container and microwave on Medium for 30 seconds, stir and repeat for another 20 seconds.

stir until ganache is smooth and glossy. Cool a little.

remove custards from refrigerator.

pour about 1 tablespoon of ganache onto each custard and smooth with the back of a spoon, leaving a small rim of custard exposed.

return desserts to refrigerator.

pouring custard (quick method)

Known as Crème Anglaise, this is a rich, thin sauce to serve with dessert cakes, puddings, meringues and fruit desserts.

1 cup milk (or use ½ milk and ½ cream)

3 eggs (59g), yolks only

1-2 tablespoons caster sugar (or to taste)

vanilla essence

place milk in a micro-safe jug and microwave on High for 2 minutes.

beat egg yolks and sugar together in a micro-safe container.

whisk warm milk into the yolk mixture using a hand-held electric blender or whisk.

return custard to microwave and cook on Medium for 1 minute.

whisk again.

repeat this step twice more or until custard begins to thicken (this may take longer if milk is taken straight from refrigerator).

add a few drops of vanilla essence to taste and whisk again.

press plastic wrap gently over surface of custard to prevent a skin forming.

refrigerate when cool. Custard will continue to thicken in the fridge.

shared secrets

For liqueur custard add 1 tablespoon Grand Marnier or Cointreau.

Custard may be prepared 1-3 days in advance.

Custard may be reheated on Medium for 1-2 minutes before serving. Whisk again.

If custard becomes too thick or lumpy whizz it in a food processor

tropical trifle with passionfruit sauce

This dessert is the perfect finish to a lazy, summer lunch with no last minute preparation required.

Serves 6

Makes 1 large bowl, or alternatively prepare individual desserts in stylish glasses.

sponge cake *(page 63)*

lime curd *(page 44)*

passionfruit sauce *(page 41) double quantity*

Kirsch (optional)

¾ cup cream, lightly whipped

2 or 3 large ripe mangoes, peeled and cut into small dice

additional ingredients

extra softly whipped cream to serve (optional)

shared secrets

Sponge cake may be made in advance and frozen until required.

Lime curd may be made up to 5 days in advance.

Passionfruit sauce may be made up to 5 days in advance.

Bananas may also be incorporated in the trifle.

Trifle best prepared several hours before eating.

prepare sponge cake. The sponge is best made the previous day, otherwise it will be too fresh to cut into cubes. You will only require about half the sponge, so freeze the remainder for another dessert.

prepare lime curd.

prepare passionfruit sauce.

cut sponge into small cubes.

sprinkle with a few teaspoons of Kirsch.

fold whipped cream into curd.

begin layering with one-third each of sponge cubes, lightened curd and mango.

drizzle with a little passionfruit sauce.

repeat layering twice more.

serve with softly whipped cream and remaining passionfruit sauce, if desired.

tiramisu (pick-me-up)

This dessert is stunning and sophisticated, yet ever so simple to prepare. Occasionally, forget the calories and indulge! I like to prepare individual desserts in elegant glasses.

Serves 4 x 250ml glasses

savoiardi *(page 35). For each dessert you will need 3-4 savoiardi.*

1 cup cold strong black coffee

5 tablespoons (3 + 2) Kahlua (coffee liqueur)

1 cup cream

3 tablespoons caster sugar

vanilla essence

1 cup mascarpone

50g quality dark chocolate, grated

prepare savoiardi.

mix prepared coffee with 3 tablespoons Kahlua in a shallow bowl. Set aside.

beat cream, sugar and a few drops of vanilla essence in the small bowl of an electric mixer until soft peaks form.

fold in mascarpone and remaining 2 tablespoons Kahlua. (Do not over-beat.)

break savoiardi in halves or to fit the glasses. Do this as you layer ingredients.

dip broken savoiardi briefly into coffee mixture and place in the base of each glass.

spoon in some mascarpone cream and level with the back of a spoon.

sprinkle with grated chocolate.

repeat layering of savoiardi, mascarpone cream and grated chocolate until you have used all ingredients.

refrigerate for several hours before serving.

shared secrets

Savoiardi may be prepared 2 weeks in advance and stored in an airtight container.

Savoiardi alternative - use stale, cubed sponge cake. If you are using sponge cake instead of savoiardi, place cubes into glasses before drizzling with the coffee/liqueur mixture.

variations

1. chocolate mocha cream
Prepare mascarpone cream as above and sift in 1 tablespoon Dutch style cocoa. Beat to combine. Layer ingredients into glasses, as above. Dust with cocoa powder or sprinkle with grated chocolate.

2. orange mascarpone cream with berries
Prepare mascarpone cream replacing Kahlua with Cointreau or Grand Marnier. Layer in glasses with raspberries or mixed fresh berries. Serve savoiardi separately, if desired.

proper custard (quick method)

Known as Crème Patissiere, this custard can be used to fill choux pastries, as a base for fruit tarts and also as a filling for sponge cakes.

2 eggs (59g), yolks only

1-2 tablespoons caster sugar

2 tablespoons + 1 teaspoon maize cornflour

300ml milk

3 teaspoons unsalted butter

vanilla essence

additional ingredients

*½ cup cream (optional - see **shared secrets**)*

mix yolks, sugar and cornflour to a paste with 2 tablespoons of the milk. Stir well.

heat remainder of milk in a micro-safe jug on High for 1 minute.

whisk warm milk into the paste using a hand-held electric blender or wire whisk.

return custard to microwave and cook on Medium for 2 minutes.

whisk again and microwave on Medium for another 1-2 minutes until custard thickens. This may take longer if milk is taken straight from refrigerator.

add butter and a few drops of vanilla essence to taste.

whisk again.

press plastic wrap gently over surface of custard to prevent a skin forming.

shared secrets

Custard can be prepared 1-3 days in advance.

To lighten the cooled custard, fold through ½ cup of whipped cream.

If custard becomes too thick or lumpy, whizz it in a food processor until smooth.

Freeze egg whites for later use.

fruit desserts

'v' indicates variation

berries with balsamic vinegar

Use seasonal berries when they are at their best for this unusual but simple dessert.

rinse hull and slice 1 or 2 punnets strawberries and place in a bowl.

sprinkle with caster sugar, drizzle with balsamic vinegar and a grinding of black pepper.

turn fruit gently with a large metal spoon and marinate for 30 minutes.

serve with **savoiardi** (page 35), a dollop of whipped cream or mascarpone.

berries with Crème de Framboise

rinse 1 or 2 punnets of fresh raspberries and place in a bowl.

sprinkle with caster sugar.

add a good splash of Crème de Framboise and marinate for 30 minutes.

serve over gluten free vanilla ice cream.

berries layered with cheat's custard

prepare glossy mixed berries (page 99).

prepare cheat's custard (page 85).

cool berries and custard.

whip 300ml cream until thick.

layer berries, custard and whipped cream in parfait glasses.

refrigerate for an hour or two.

serve with **savoiardi** (page 35).

glossy mixed berries over ice cream

Any combination of berries may be used for this summery dessert. If fresh raspberries and blueberries are not available use frozen berries. This recipe can be served with panna cotta, meringues or layered in trifles with cake and custard.

Serves 6

150g each of fresh strawberries, raspberries and blueberries

⅓ cup pure icing sugar

¼ cup boiling water

¼ cup Kirsch, Crème de Framboise or orange-flavoured liqueur

3 teaspoons arrowroot

2 tablespoons cold water

1 teaspoon lemon juice

finely grated zest of 1 lemon

additional ingredients
vanilla ice cream, gluten free

rinse and hull strawberries, cut in half if they are large. Pick over, rinse remaining berries and place in a bowl.

sprinkle icing sugar over berries.

pour boiling water and liqueur over berries and turn gently. Marinate for 30 minutes.

strain berries over a saucepan to catch the syrup. Reserve the berries and syrup.

mix arrowroot to a paste with the 2 tablespoons cold water.

stir lemon juice, zest and arrowroot paste into reserved syrup.

heat gently, whisking continuously until syrup thickens.

remove saucepan from heat and pour thickened syrup over reserved berries.

fold berries gently through syrup.

serve cooled over ice cream.

shared secrets

Berries may be prepared in advance and will keep well for several days.

Frozen berries do not need to be rinsed.

rockmelon and raspberries

This is a super-easy summer sweet. Cream is unnecessary but the choice is yours.

Serves 2

1 very small rockmelon
1 punnet of raspberries
2 tablespoons caster sugar
1 tablespoon lime juice

peel rockmelon and cut it in half. Remove seeds.

place raspberries in a bowl.

sprinkle with sugar and lime juice.

allow to marinate for 10 minutes.

to serve

place rockmelon halves into bowls.

fill the cavity with marinated raspberries.

shared secrets

Prepare fruit close to serving time.

Melon can also be cut in wedges and served on dessert plates with marinated raspberries.

Rockmelon is also delicious served with fresh passionfruit and softly whipped cream.

peaches with raspberries

Summertime means delectable stone fruits to me. Purchase fragrant peaches when they are at their best and avoid hard unripe fruit.

Serves 4

2 large freestone peaches

1 punnet of raspberries

raspberry liqueur (Crème de Framboise)

cream, lightly whipped

blanch peaches in boiling water for a minute or so to remove skins.

hold peaches gently with a clean cloth (this is to prevent the peach from slipping).

cut peaches in half and twist to remove the stone.

place peach halves in dessert bowls and spoon raspberries into the cavity.

drizzle with raspberry liqueur and serve with cream.

shared secrets

Best prepared close to serving time.

If raspberries need to be sweetened, sprinkle with pure icing sugar before drizzling with liqueur.

mango and blueberries

Use only fresh blueberries for this simple yet delicious summer dessert.

Serves 4

2 large mangoes

1 punnet of fresh blueberries

1 large orange, strained juice only

1 tablespoon caster sugar

additional ingredients

vanilla ice cream, gluten free

peel mangoes, cut the cheeks into slices. Set aside.

rinse a punnet of blueberries and remove any stems. Prick 10 berries with a skewer.

combine orange juice and sugar in a small saucepan and heat to dissolve sugar.

add blueberries and gently swirl over low heat until berries soften slightly and release some of their colour. Their skins should remain intact. Do not be tempted to overcook the blueberries as the skin will split.

cool berries in the liquid. (As they cool the colour will intensify.)

remove berries using a slotted spoon and boil the liquid to reduce to 2 tablespoons.

pour reduced syrup back over berries.

serve mango, blueberries and syrup with ice cream.

shared secrets

Prepare blueberries on the day.

Cut mango just prior to serving.

melon with kaffir lime and mint sherbet

This is a zingy, refreshing, light summer dessert. Recipe can be doubled. Serve in stemmed dessert glasses.

Makes 4 small scoops

for the melon
1 small ripe rockmelon

1 small ripe honeydew or champagne melon

for the sherbet
½ cup caster sugar

1 cup water

2 or 3 kaffir lime leaves

2 limes, zest and ½ cup lime juice

1 cup firmly packed mint leaves (chopped)

⅓ cup Greek style yogurt

1 egg (59g), white only

additional ingredients
kaffir lime leaves to garnish

shared secrets
Sherbet may be made well in advance and served straight from the freezer.

Serve sherbet with mixed berries instead of melon.

Substitute lemons for limes.

Kaffir lime leaves may be frozen.

to prepare melons
scoop small balls of melon using a melon baller and place them in a bowl.

cover with plastic wrap and refrigerate until serving time.

for the sherbet
simmer sugar, water and lime leaves for 3 or 4 minutes or until sugar dissolves.

place zest, lime juice and chopped mint leaves in a bowl.

pour hot syrup over and allow to cool completely.

strain, pressing down on the leaves. Discard zest, mint and lime leaves. Strain syrup again using a very fine sieve.

freeze until firm then allow to soften enough to break up.

transfer to a food processor and whizz for a few seconds.

add yogurt and whizz to blend. Transfer to a shallow container and place in the freezer while you whip the egg white.

whip egg white in a small mixing bowl until soft peaks form.

fold egg white into sherbet using a wire whisk.

transfer back into the shallow container.

freeze until firm then break up and process again.

transfer back into the shallow container.

refreeze until you are ready to serve.

to serve
place a combination of melon balls into stemmed dessert glasses.

scoop sherbet on top and garnish with a lime leaf.

oven baked rhubarb

Cooking rhubarb by this method is quick and easy.

Grease a casserole dish with a lid that is large enough to hold the rhubarb.

preheat oven to 170°C

1kg rhubarb
½ cup caster sugar
½ cup light brown sugar
1 orange, grated zest and strained juice

prepare rhubarb by rinsing it well. Trim, cut into 4cm lengths and place in casserole dish.

sprinkle sugars and zest over rhubarb and mix to coat.

pour orange juice over rhubarb.

cover and bake undisturbed for about 35-45 minutes or until rhubarb has softened, but still holds its shape.

variation
oven baked rhubarb crumble

prepare crumble as per **crumbly apple tart** (page 151).

remove some syrup from prepared rhubarb. (This is so the crumble sits on top of the rhubarb, not in the syrup.)

sprinkle crumble over rhubarb.

bake in a preheated oven at 180°C until crumble turns light golden brown.

shared secrets

Oven baked rhubarb will keep for several days in the refrigerator.

Cooked rhubarb freezes well and will keep for up to 3 months.

ruby poached pears

These peppery poached pears make such an elegant, sensuous dessert. They can be prepared in advance and served with a minimum of fuss. If pears are small serve whole.

Serves 4-6

for the poaching syrup

note: If cooking whole pears make 1½ times the quantity of syrup.

1 cup water

1 cup sugar

1 cup red wine

1 cinnamon stick

5 whole black peppercorns

1 strip of orange rind (remove any white pith)

for the pears

6 small whole pears or 4 large pears (beurre bosc)

additional ingredients (optional)
honey panna cotta *(page 87)*

cream

pouring custard (quick method) *(page 92)*

shared secrets
Best prepared on the day, but pears will keep well for two days.

The slower you cook pears the more the flavour will develop.

for the poaching syrup

choose a heavy-based frypan or saucepan that will hold pears in a single layer.

combine poaching ingredients, bring to the boil then simmer until sugar dissolves. Remove from heat.

for the pears

peel pears and cut in half if large, or if cooking whole pears peel and cut a thin slice off the base of each pear so that they will not fall over in the syrup while cooking.

scoop the core out of halved pears using a melon baller or small rounded spoon.

remove core end by cutting a small 'V' either side of it. Leave stem attached to half of pear if you wish.

place prepared pears directly into the syrup.

simmer pears slowly until tender, about 1 hour depending on ripeness of the fruit.

roll pears over every 10 minutes to ensure they cook evenly.

spoon syrup over pears often. When pears have turned a ruby colour, test with a skewer. It should slide into the flesh without resistance.

remove pears carefully to a bowl.

reduce syrup by boiling vigorously for about 5 minutes then pour over pears.

serve with **honey panna cotta**, cream or **pouring custard (quick method)**

syrupy satsuma plums

I adore the fruits of summer, especially Satsuma plums. They are great served over ice cream, in tarts or with **honey panna cotta** (page 87). Do not use over-ripe fruit for this recipe.

Serves 4-6

1 cup water

½ cup sugar

12 ripe Satsuma plums, cut in half and stones removed

place water and sugar in a large frypan, one that will hold the fruit in a single layer.

heat on high until water boils and sugar dissolves. Turn down heat to a gentle simmer.

add plums, all facing cut side up.

simmer for 5 minutes.

turn plums over and cook another 5 minutes.

repeat twice more (total 20 minutes cooking time). I like the fruit to maintain its shape rather than collapsing.

remove fruit to another container using a slotted spoon.

reduce syrup by boiling it vigorously for about 5-7 minutes.

pour reduced syrup over plums.

refrigerate when cool.

meringue
desserts

'v' indicates variation

mighty meringue or the ever popular pavlova

Who can resist this good old Aussie favourite? Lightly crisp on the outside yet soft and marshmallow like inside.

Serves 6-8

Draw a 22cm circle onto baking paper. To avoid pencil marks on base of meringue, reverse paper before placing on baking tray. Alternatively, pavlova may be baked in a 22cm square cake tin. Line base and sides with baking paper (see **shared secrets** over page).

preheat oven to 120°C

*4 eggs (59g), whites only **(eggs must be at room temperature)***

¼ teaspoon cream of tartar

1 cup caster sugar

2 teaspoons maize cornflour

1 teaspoon white wine vinegar

additional ingredients

whipped cream

fresh berries or banana to serve

***passionfruit sauce** (page 41)*

beat egg whites and cream of tartar in the small bowl of an electric mixer until soft peaks form. (See **shared secrets** over page.)

add ⅓ cup sugar and beat for 3 minutes.

add remainder of sugar 1 tablespoon at a time, beating well between additions until sugar dissolves. Rub a little meringue between thumb and finger. If the texture is still grainy, it means the sugar has not dissolved, so continue beating until dissolved. The meringue should look shiny and thick.

sift cornflour over meringue using a tea strainer.

add vinegar and fold in gently.

spread mixture onto prepared tray/tin. Smooth off the surface.

bake for 1¼ hours then turn oven off and leave door shut for one hour (this will help prevent cracking).

serve with whipped cream and fresh berries or bananas and **passionfruit sauce**.

for individual pavlovas

preheat oven to 120°C

using two large spoons, heap 6-8 spoonfuls of meringue onto baking paper and draw it up into peaks.

bake for about 45 minutes or until dry.

continued on next page

to make individual pavlovas using an egg ring

You will get nine 7cm egg ring size pavlovas from ½ quantity of **mighty meringue** mixture.

Line a baking tray with baking paper.

place egg ring onto baking paper.

fill egg ring with meringue mixture and even it off with a flat knife.

using the base of a wine glass that is slightly smaller than the egg ring, lightly press down on the meringue.

lift ring off tray and up the stem of the glass. The meringue will stick to the base of the glass. Use a knife to separate meringue from the glass. It's a bit tricky but practice makes perfect.

repeat until you have used all the meringue.

bake as for individual pavlovas and decorate as desired.

variations

1. chocolate meringues
sift 2 tablespoons Dutch style cocoa with the cornflour and fold into the meringue.

2. nutty chocolate meringues
sift 2 tablespoons Dutch style cocoa with the cornflour and fold into the meringue. Add ¼ cup flaked, blanched almonds or ground hazelnuts and fold in lightly.

3. coconut meringues
after sifting in the cornflour, lightly fold ½ cup shredded coconut into the meringue.

shared secrets

When whisking egg whites, choose a perfectly clean small mixing bowl. Eggs must be at room temperature. Begin whisking whites slowly, then as they begin to froth, increase the speed. The volume of the whites will increase considerably.

If you have baked the pavlova in a cake tin, place a piece of baking paper onto a wire rack before turning it out.

walnut flans with banana, sour cream and caramel sauce

Serves 8

Generously grease eight 8cm x 2cm flan tins with removable bases.

preheat oven to 180°C

for the flans

1 cup gluten free breadcrumbs

4 eggs (59g), whites only

1 cup caster sugar

1 cup walnuts, finely chopped, but still with a bit of texture

additional ingredients

400ml thick sour cream

4 perfectly ripe bananas

1 lemon, juice only

caramel sauce *(page 42)*

extra chopped walnuts to garnish

shared secrets

Flans may be frozen.

Flans can be prepared several days in advance and stored in an airtight container.

Substitute sweet gluten free biscuit crumbs in place of breadcrumbs.

for the flans

place breadcrumbs on a baking tray and dry in oven until crisp but not too brown.

beat egg whites until soft peaks form.

add sugar gradually, about a tablespoon at a time, beating well until sugar dissolves.

mix breadcrumbs and walnuts together and fold through beaten whites using a large metal spoon.

spoon mixture into flan tins and lightly even the surface with a flat knife.

bake for about 15-20 minutes or until lightly browned.

cool on a wire rack for 10 minutes before removing from tins. (Do not be concerned if tops crack a little as they will be coated with sour cream.)

prepare caramel sauce.

to serve

spread tops of cooled flans with sour cream and place on dessert plates.

slice bananas and dip into lemon juice.

overlap banana slices around edge of flans.

drizzle caramel sauce over bananas, allowing some to run onto the plates.

scatter with extra chopped walnuts.

meringue crush with mixed berries

Makes 6-8 individual desserts

petite meringues *(page 31)*
cheat's custard *(page 85)*
glossy mixed berries *(page 99)*
300ml cream, lightly whipped

prepare petite meringues.

prepare cheat's custard and cool.

prepare glossy mixed berries and cool.

to serve

break meringue into bite-size pieces.

layer custard, meringue, cream and berries in individual glasses.

repeat layering to the top of glasses, finishing with berries.

refrigerate for up to 2 hours before serving.

shared secrets
Meringues may be prepared a day in advance and stored in an airtight container.

Berries may be prepared and refrigerated several days in advance.

macaroon and raspberry ice cream terrine

After eating this terrine, my friend said, "I could live on that dessert!" What a compliment.

This terrine is great for a crowd as it can be prepared in advance and sliced ready to plate just before eating. The recipe looks long but can be prepared in stages. The process is quite simple if you follow my instructions carefully.

Serves 10

Prepare baking paper for macaroon layers by drawing three rectangles measuring 7cm x 25cm. Leave room for layers to spread a little. To avoid pencil marks on macaroon layers, reverse drawn side of paper before placing on baking tray.

preheat oven to 140°C

for the macaroon layers

½ cup blanched ground almonds or almond meal

½ cup desiccated coconut

1 teaspoon maize cornflour

2 eggs (59g), whites only

½ cup caster sugar

1 teaspoon white wine vinegar

additional ingredients

1 litre vanilla ice cream, gluten free

*2 cups **raspberry sauce** (page 41) (1 cup for the berry ice cream and 1 cup for serving)*

500ml whipped cream for assembling and 'icing' terrine

1-2 cups shredded coconut

combine almonds, coconut and cornflour in a bowl.

beat egg whites until soft peaks form, then gradually add sugar a tablespoon at a time, beating until sugar dissolves.

add vinegar.

fold in combined almond mixture.

spread a third of the mixture onto each rectangle, keeping within the lines. Smooth tops of the layers.

bake for about 35-40 minutes or until macaroon layers are pale, firm and crisp.

cool on a wire rack. Remove baking paper when layers are cool.

store macaroon layers in an airtight container until you are ready to assemble terrine.

for the berry ice cream layers

line a shallow rectangular cake tin measuring approximately 18cm x 28cm with freezer wrap, allowing plenty of overhang. (When you come to assemble the terrine you will be able to trim ice cream and macaroon layers to the same size, if necessary.)

allow ice cream to soften slightly.

continued on next page

scoop small spoonfuls of ice cream and place into lined cake tin. It should look uneven.

spoon or pour **1 cup only** of raspberry sauce over ice cream, letting it settle in the cracks.

fold overhanging wrap over top of the ice cream and press down gently and evenly with your hands until ice cream is level.

freeze berry ice cream until firm.

to assemble the terrine

unwrap berry ice cream and place on a cutting board.

cut ice cream in half lengthwise, so that you have two slices measuring the same size as the macaroon layers. Trim to size if necessary.

place one macaroon layer on a board or tray that will fit into your freezer.

spread macaroon layer with a thin coating of whipped cream and place a slice of ice cream on top.

spread both sides of the middle macaroon layer with cream and place on top of ice cream.

place the second slice of ice cream on top.

spread third macaroon layer with a thin coating of cream and place on top of ice cream.

return assembled terrine to the freezer until very firm before 'icing'.

for the 'icing'

spread the top and one side of terrine with whipped cream and sprinkle with coconut.

place terrine in freezer for about half an hour or until cream is firm.

repeat above step on the other sides of terrine.

place terrine back in freezer until you are ready to serve.

serve terrine cut into 2cm wide slices. Place on large dessert plates and serve with some reserved raspberry sauce.

shared secrets

Substitute strawberry sauce for raspberry sauce.

The macaroon layers may be prepared 2 days in advance.

Raspberry sauce may be made a week in advance, refrigerated and/or frozen.

Cut terrine in portions up to 3 hours before required. Return cut slices to freezer.

The terrine will keep well for a week.

mousses, a jelly & a couple of fools

'v' indicates variation

light and fluffy passionfruit mousse

Passionfruit is an astringent fruit with a wonderful heady fragrance. It blends beautifully with softly whipped cream as in this mousse.

Serve mousse in a large bowl or individual dessert glasses.

Serves 4-6

½ cup passionfruit pulp (about
  6 whole passionfruit)

½ cup caster sugar

¼ cup water

2 oranges, strained juice only

1 lime or lemon, strained juice only

1 tablespoon gluten free custard
  powder

2 eggs (59g), separated

2 teaspoons gelatine

2 tablespoons warm water

1 cup cream, lightly whipped

additional ingredients
extra whipped cream (optional)

3 passionfruit or **passionfruit sauce**
  (page 41)

simmer passionfruit pulp, sugar and water in a small saucepan, just long enough to dissolve the sugar.

strain syrup and return it to the saucepan along with 1 tablespoon of passionfruit seeds. Discard remainder of seeds.

blend orange juice, lime or lemon juice, custard powder and egg yolks together in a small bowl.

add to passionfruit syrup. Stir well.

heat mixture gently and whisk until slightly thickened. Set aside.

sprinkle gelatine over warm water and microwave on Medium for 30 seconds or until dissolved.

stir dissolved gelatine into custard.

cool custard slightly by resting saucepan in cold water in the sink.

whip egg whites until soft peaks form.

fold whites into whipped cream, then into cooled passionfruit custard.

pour into a large bowl or individual glasses.

refrigerate for several hours.

garnish with cream and passionfruit or **passionfruit sauce**.

shared secrets
Mousse is best prepared and eaten on the day.

Freeze passionfruit pulp in ice cube trays.

mango mousse

When I see the first mangoes in the market in October it's a reminder that summer is just around the corner. Ripe mango is sweet, tender and succulent.

Makes 4 x 200ml glasses

2 large ripe mangoes

¼ cup caster sugar (if mango is very ripe, use less sugar)

1 lemon or lime, strained juice and finely grated zest

1½ teaspoons gelatine

2 tablespoons warm water

2 eggs (59g), whites only

⅔ cup cream, lightly whipped

additional ingredients
extra whipped cream

1 mango and 2 passionfruit to garnish

peel mangoes and cut flesh from the stone.

puree mango flesh, sugar, juice and zest in a food processor.

sprinkle gelatine over warm water and microwave on Medium for 30 seconds or until dissolved.

add gelatine to mango mixture and whizz to blend.

whip egg whites until soft peaks form.

fold whites into whipped cream and then into mango puree.

spoon into glasses.

refrigerate for several hours.

serve with a dollop of cream, sliced mango and passionfruit.

shared secrets

Mousse is best prepared and eaten on the day.

Frozen mango whilst not ideal, may be used in this dessert.

citrus berry mousse

Serve mousse in a large glass bowl or prepare individual desserts.

Serves 8

for the berry puree
125g raspberries
125g strawberries

for the mousse
3 eggs (59g), separated
½ cup caster sugar
2 tablespoons strained lemon or lime juice
finely grated zest of 1 lemon or lime
2 teaspoons gelatine
2 tablespoons warm water
300ml cream, lightly whipped

additional ingredients
extra strawberries to garnish (optional)

shared secret
Best prepared and eaten on the day.

for the berry puree

puree berries in a food processor.

strain through a sieve to remove seeds. Discard seeds.

divide puree into two, reserving half to serve with the mousse.

for the mousse

place yolks, sugar, juice and zest into a stainless steel bowl and whisk over simmering water until thick and creamy.

remove from heat and cool slightly. Stir occasionally.

sprinkle gelatine over warm water and microwave on Medium for 30 seconds or until dissolved.

stir into the cooling custard.

whip egg whites until soft peaks form.

fold egg whites into whipped cream and then into the custard.

swirl half the berry puree through the mousse. Do not over-stir as mousse should have a marbled appearance.

pour into a glass bowl or individual dessert glasses.

refrigerate for several hours.

serve mousse drizzled with reserved berry puree and extra strawberries.

gin and ruby grapefruit jelly with tropical salsa

The juniper berry tang of gin and tonic had always been a favourite cocktail drink of mine until my friend Jane introduced me to gin and ruby pink grapefruit juice. So I decided not only to drink it but created this very delicate dessert to savour the taste. I think the Queen Mother would have approved!

Set the jelly in martini glasses for a touch of elegance.

Serves 4

for the jelly

2 cups Ruby Grapefruit Juice (Ocean Spray brand) at room temperature

1 tablespoon gelatine

3 tablespoons warm water

3 tablespoons Bombay Sapphire Gin

1 tablespoon strained lemon juice or lime juice

for the tropical salsa

The salsa should look delicate so cut fruit into very small dice 5mm approximately, in size.

1 kiwi fruit

½ cup chopped pineapple or mango

4 strawberries, rinsed and hulled

½ ruby grapefruit

2 teaspoons caster sugar or to taste

1 nip of gin

mint leaves to garnish

for the jelly

strain grapefruit juice into a small micro-safe jug and microwave on Medium for 2 minutes (3 minutes if grapefruit juice is used straight from the refrigerator).

sprinkle gelatine over warm water and microwave on Medium for 40-50 seconds or until dissolved.

stir gelatine into warmed grapefruit juice.

add gin and lemon juice. Stir well.

place glasses on a tray and pour in the liquid. Refrigerate for several hours.

remove from refrigerator about half an hour before serving.

serve jelly with a large spoonful of salsa and garnish with mint leaves.

for the tropical salsa

remove skin from fruit and pith from grapefruit.

cut all fruit into very small dice, approximately 5mm in size and combine.

sprinkle with sugar and gin.

shared secrets

Jelly may be prepared a day in advance.

Fruit best prepared on the day.

Cream is not necessary with this dessert.

dried apricot fool

So easy any fool can do it! This is another dessert that can be made year round as dried apricots are always available. My friend Helen suggested the variation **frozen apricot fool**. This dessert is a summer addiction of ours!

Serves 4-6

230g dried apricots

¼ cup sugar

1 cup water

¼ cup brandy or orange liqueur

½ cup Greek style yogurt

1 cup cream, whipped

additional ingredients (optional)
apricot sauce *(page 41)*

place apricots, sugar, water and brandy in a **deep** micro-safe container.

cover with plastic wrap and microwave on High for 4 minutes, stir. Re-cover with plastic wrap and microwave for another 4 minutes. Carefully remove plastic wrap.

remove 12 apricot halves and some syrup for the garnish. Set aside.

puree remaining apricots and liquid in a food processor. Allow to cool.

add yogurt to food processor and whizz to combine.

swirl apricot/yogurt mixture through whipped cream, giving it a marbled appearance.

spoon into dessert bowls or elegant glasses.

chill for several hours in the refrigerator.

serve each dessert garnished with 2 reserved apricots and a little syrup.

continued on next page

variation

frozen apricot fool

Serves 6

Line six 120ml timbale moulds with freezer wrap, leaving plenty of overhang.

prepare dried apricot fool recipe on previous page.

spoon mixture into moulds and smooth tops.

fold overhang to cover the tops.

freeze for several hours until firm.

remove moulds from freezer to refrigerator half an hour before serving. This is to allow the frozen fools to soften slightly.

to serve

remove freezer wrap from moulds.

place frozen fools onto dessert plates.

top each with 2 reserved apricots and drizzle with syrup.

For a jazzy presentation serve frozen apricot fool with **apricot sauce**.

place apricot sauce into a plastic sauce bottle and as you squeeze, zigzag sauce across one side of the plate.

shared secrets
Fool is best prepared several hours prior to eating.

plum fool

The recipe uses 12 plums. You will require 6 in the fool and 6 to serve with the fool.

Serves 6

syrupy satsuma plums (page 110)

2 cups cream

2 tablespoons pure icing sugar

prepare syrupy satsuma plums.

remove skin from 6 plums and drain well on paper towels.

puree plums in a food processor.

place cream in the small bowl of an electric mixer, sift icing sugar over and whip until firm.

swirl plum puree through whipped cream.

spoon into dessert bowls or elegant glasses.

refrigerate for several hours.

serve with remaining **syrupy satsuma plums**.

shared secrets

Add more icing sugar to taste, if plums are not sweet enough.

Fool is best prepared several hours prior to eating.

Instead of 2 cups cream substitute 1 cup smooth ricotta and 1 cup cream.

mango fool

Serves 6

2 large ripe mangoes

2 tablespoons strained lemon or lime juice

1 cup cream

1 or 2 tablespoons pure icing sugar (or to taste, depending on ripeness of mango)

½ cup Greek style yogurt

2 passionfruit (optional)

additional ingredients

mango and/or passionfruit to garnish

almond bread (page 9) (optional)

peel mangoes and cut flesh from stone.

puree mango flesh and juice in a food processor.

place cream in the small bowl of an electric mixer, sift icing sugar over and beat until firm.

fold in yogurt.

stir in mango puree and passionfruit pulp.

spoon into dessert bowls or elegant glasses.

refrigerate for several hours.

serve fool garnished with sliced mango and/or passionfruit and **almond bread**.

shared secret
Fool is best prepared several hours prior to eating.

puddings

apple and hazelnut clafouti

This is a light version of the French classic. Apricots or pitted cherries may be substituted.

Serves 4-6

Grease a 23cm pie dish or prepare 6 individual 11cm x 2.5cm ovenproof dishes. I think individual desserts make a better presentation.

preheat oven to 170°C

for the apples

4 large cooking apples

¼ cup caster sugar

1 lemon, finely grated zest and strained juice

1 tablespoon brandy or Calvados

25g unsalted butter

for the custard batter

2 eggs (59g)

2 tablespoons caster sugar

⅓ cup milk

⅔ cup cream

vanilla essence

2 tablespoons gluten free self raising flour

⅓ cup ground hazelnuts

additional ingredients

caster sugar (optional)

cream to serve

shared secrets

Apples may be prepared and cooked in advance.

Clafouti is best eaten soon after baking.

for the apples

peel, core and cut apples into 1cm cubes.

combine apples, sugar, zest, juice and brandy in a bowl.

melt butter in a frypan and add sugar coated apples.

cook on high heat for about 5 minutes, moving apples around continuously until the liquid has evaporated.

remove from heat when apples are just cooked.

spoon apples into ovenproof dish/es and place on a flat baking tray.

for the custard batter

place eggs, sugar, milk, cream and a few drops of vanilla essence into a food processor and blend well.

sift flour and add to processor. Whizz until custard batter is smooth.

add ground hazelnuts and whizz briefly. Scrape down sides of food processor.

pour batter over apples.

bake for about 25-35 minutes for individual dishes or longer for one large dish. The top should be golden and custard batter set. Test with a skewer which should come out clean.

sprinkle with caster sugar and pop under the grill briefly.

serve hot or warm with cream.

apricot bread and butter puddings

Serves 6

Grease 6 x 200ml ovenproof dishes or you can make one large dish.

preheat oven to 170°C

for the apricots

150g dried apricots

¼ cup sugar

¾ cup water

for the puddings

8 small thin slices of gluten free bread

30g soft unsalted butter, approximately

1 cup milk

1 cup cream

3 eggs (59g)

2 tablespoons caster sugar

vanilla essence

ground nutmeg to finish

additional ingredients

cream to serve

shared secret

Best prepared on the day and eaten soon after baking.

for the apricots

place apricots, sugar and water in a **deep** micro-safe container.

cover with plastic wrap and microwave on High for 4 minutes, stir. Re-cover with plastic wrap and microwave for another 3 minutes. Carefully remove plastic wrap.

for the puddings

lightly butter both sides of bread, remove crusts and cut into 1cm cubes or triangles.

divide bread and apricots between dishes, making sure some apricots are exposed on top.

combine milk and cream in a micro-safe container and microwave on High for 3 minutes.

whisk eggs and sugar together in a large bowl.

pour warmed milk mixture over eggs and sugar, whisking well to combine.

add a few drops of vanilla essence.

strain liquid into a jug and pour over bread and apricots.

allow to stand for 20 minutes then top up with custard if necessary.

dust with nutmeg.

bake for 25-30 minutes or until set and golden brown. Bake longer for a large dish.

serve with softly whipped cream.

pear and pecan upside down puddings

This is a perfect winter pudding. It is not too rich or heavy. Apples or poached quince may be substituted.

Serves 6

Generously grease 6 x 8cm individual pie tins and line bases with greased baking paper.

preheat oven to 180°C

for the pears

30 pecan nuts (5 per tin)

3 small firm pears (beurre bosc)

50g unsalted butter

⅓ cup brown sugar

1 tablespoon water

for the puddings

¼ cup golden syrup

30ml milk

50g unsalted butter

¼ cup brown sugar

1 egg (59g)

¾ cup gluten free self raising flour

1 teaspoon ground ginger or cinnamon

additional ingredients

caramel sauce *(page 42)*

cream to serve

shared secrets

Puddings may be prepared a day in advance.

Reheat in a microwave on Medium for about 30 seconds or until warm.

Puddings can be frozen.

for the pears

place pecan nuts around the base of each tin with the flat surface of the nut facing up.

peel, core and cut pears into 5mm slices.

combine butter, sugar and water in a frypan and heat until butter melts.

add pears and cook over medium heat until fruit is cooked. Turn fruit during cooking.

cool for 5 minutes.

drizzle some caramel from pan into the base of each tin.

arrange pears slightly overlapping on the caramel.

for the puddings

place golden syrup and milk in a micro-safe container and microwave on Medium for 1 minute, stir to blend and set aside.

cream butter and sugar in the small bowl of an electric mixer until pale and thick.

add egg and beat well, scraping down sides of bowl.

sift flour and spice together.

fold flour and reserved liquid into creamed mixture.

spoon pudding batter over pears.

bake for 20-25 minutes or until a skewer inserted into the centre comes out clean.

cool in tins for 5 minutes before gently turning out onto a wire rack.

prepare caramel sauce.

serve with whipped cream and **caramel sauce**.

luscious lemon puddings

As lemons are always available, this dessert is not reliant on a particular season, so they can be enjoyed at any time of the year. This spongy pudding has a lemon curd-like sauce underneath. It is more like a soufflé than a pudding—light and luscious.

Serves 6

Grease six 200ml pudding moulds.

preheat oven to 180°C

50g unsalted butter

⅓ cup + 1 tablespoon caster sugar

2 eggs (59g), separated

1 tablespoon gluten free self raising flour

1 tablespoon white rice flour

1 cup milk

2 large lemons, finely grated zest and ⅓ cup of strained juice

additional ingredients

pure icing sugar

pouring cream to serve

shared secrets

Best prepared on the day and eaten soon after baking.

Substitute limes for lemons.

Grated lemon or lime zest can be sprinkled over puddings before baking.

Leftover puddings may be reheated in a microwave oven on Medium for a minute. They will have shrunk a little but still taste good.

To maximise lemon and lime juice, microwave lemon or lime on High for 30 seconds.

cream butter and ⅓ cup sugar in a food processor.

add yolks and blend.

sift flours together and add alternately with milk to make a smooth batter. Scrape down sides of processor.

blend in zest and lemon juice.

beat egg whites in the small bowl of an electric mixer until soft peaks form.

add extra tablespoon of caster sugar gradually, beating until dissolved.

pour lemon batter gently into whipped whites, folding together using the lowest speed.

transfer to a jug and pour into pudding moulds.

place moulds in a bain-marie (refer note below).

bake for 25-35 minutes or until cooked. The tops should be puffed and golden.

dust with icing sugar and serve immediately with pouring cream.

note

Boil kettle before you commence recipe so that it is ready to pour into the bain-marie just before baking the puddings. (Refer **secrets for success - making and baking gluten free - bain-marie** page 7).

apple sponge puddings

These puddings are best cooked close to serving time as the sponge will deflate a little. They will, however, still taste delish.

Serves 6

Lightly grease six 250ml ovenproof dishes.

preheat oven to 180°C

for the apples

6 small cooking apples

1 lemon, finely grated zest and strained juice

¼ cup caster sugar

½ teaspoon ground cinnamon

for the sponge topping

2 tablespoons potato flour

2 tablespoons gluten free self raising flour

2 tablespoons maize cornflour

½ teaspoon gluten free baking powder

½ teaspoon ground cinnamon

2 eggs (59g)

¼ cup caster sugar

1 tablespoon boiling water

additional ingredients

pure icing sugar

pouring custard (quick method) (page 92) and/ or cream

for the apples

peel, core and cut apples into 1cm cubes and place in a bowl.

add lemon zest, juice, sugar and cinnamon. Mix to coat apples.

divide apples between dishes.

for the sponge topping

sift flours, baking powder and cinnamon together.

beat eggs and sugar in the small bowl of an electric mixer on the highest speed setting until thick and creamy. (This takes about 5 minutes.)

boil the kettle.

fold sifted mixture gently into egg mixture using low speed or a large metal spoon.

add boiling water and stir very briefly.

spoon sponge topping over apples.

bake for about 25 minutes or until sponge is lightly brown and springy to the touch.

dust with icing sugar and serve with **pouring custard (quick method)** and/or cream.

shared secrets

Add ½ cup ground almonds to apple mixture. This will give you 7 puddings.

Combine apples with berries or pears.

Vary spice if you wish.

tarts

'v' indicates variation

tips on pastry making and baking

pastry - to roll and press

My recipes for gluten free pastry may be rolled as soon as they are made. There is no need for it to rest as it contains no gluten.

Spray or lightly grease flan tin/s.

Use arrowroot flour in a shaker to dust your rolling pin and surface of bench top or board on which you roll pastry. Arrowroot prevents pastry sticking and helps to hold it together.

Both pastry recipes roll beautifully, but when lining large tart tins the pastry will tear, so simply line the tin in sections, pressing the pastry in place with your fingers, as evenly as possible.

Even off pastry by rolling the rolling pin over the top of the tin or trim evenly with a knife. Place pastry-lined tin/s into the freezer for 10-15 minutes. Freezing the uncooked pastry shell is very **important** as it will help prevent shrinkage.

Baking pastry 'blind' means to pre-bake a pastry shell before adding the filling.

NOTE: there is **NO NEED** to fill gluten free pastry lined flan tin/s with paper/foil and dried beans before pre-baking. Simply take the flan tin/s from the freezer, place on a baking tray and pre-bake.

Pre-bake pastry lined flan tin/s in a preheated oven at 190°C for 15-20 minutes, allow to cool before filling.

If cracks appear **after** baking, simply repair gently with uncooked pastry before filling.

pastry - to fill pastry cases with liquid fillings

Place pastry lined tin/s onto a flat oven tray. Half fill with liquid filling then transfer tray to the oven shelf and fill with remaining liquid. Slide tray back gently to avoid spillage.

shortcrust pastry

Refer to **tips on pastry making and baking** (page 144) before continuing.

This quantity will make one 20cm, 22cm or 23cm flan tin or 8 individual 8cm x 2cm tins.
Roll pastry out thinly.

¼ cup gluten free self raising flour

¼ cup gluten free plain flour

¼ cup maize cornflour

¼ cup white rice flour

2 tablespoons glutinous rice flour*

1 tablespoon gluten free custard
   powder

2 tablespoons caster sugar

100g soft unsalted butter

1 egg (59g)

1 teaspoon strained lemon juice

a few drops of water (if necessary)

place flours, custard powder and sugar into a food processor and whizz to combine.

add butter and process until mixture resembles coarse breadcrumbs. This will take about 10-15 seconds.

crack egg into a small jug and with a fork, whisk in lemon juice.

pour egg mixture into food processor through the feed tube with motor running.

pulse (turn on and off action). Stop food processor when the pastry comes together in a mass. DO NOT OVER-PROCESS.

add a few drops of water **only** if necessary.

remove pastry from processor and form into a flat disc if making one large flan. Alternatively, shape pastry into a short roll and cut even segments for individual flans.

reminder

refer - **tips on pastry making and baking**.

shared secret

Gluten free pastry may be rolled immediately, once made. There is no need for it to rest as it contains no gluten.

* Glutinous rice flour is available from Asian grocery stores.

rich nutty shortcrust pastry

The nuts add both texture and taste to this delicious pastry.

Refer to **tips on pastry making and baking** (page 144) before continuing.

This quantity will make one 20cm, 22cm or 23cm flan tin or 8 individual 8cm x 2cm tins.
Roll pastry out thinly.

¼ cup gluten free self raising flour
¼ cup gluten free plain flour
¼ cup maize cornflour or potato flour
¼ cup white rice flour
2 tablespoons glutinous rice flour*
2 tablespoons caster sugar
80g soft unsalted butter
¼ cup almond or hazelnut meal
1 egg (59g)
vanilla essence
1 teaspoon strained lemon juice

place flours and sugar into a food processor and whizz to combine.

add butter and process until mixture resembles coarse breadcrumbs. This will take about 10-15 seconds.

add nut meal and whizz to combine.

crack egg into a small jug and using a fork, whisk in a few drops of vanilla essence and lemon juice.

pour egg mixture into food processor through the feed tube with motor running. You may or may not require all the liquid.

pulse (turn on and off action). Stop the processor when the pastry comes together in a mass. DO NOT OVER-PROCESS.

remove pastry from processor and form it into a flat disc if making one large flan. Alternatively, shape pastry into a short roll and cut even segments for individual flans.

reminder
refer - **tips on pastry making and baking**.

shared secret
Gluten free pastry may be rolled immediately, once it is made.
There is no need for it to rest as it contains no gluten.

* Glutinous rice flour is available from Asian grocery stores.

passionfruit and citrus tart

This is a deliciously light, summer tart, and so easy to make.

Serves 6

Spray or lightly grease a 22cm or 23cm flan tin with removable base, or alternatively six individual 8cm x 2cm tins.

preheat oven to 190°C

shortcrust pastry *(page 145)*

for the filling

1 large lemon, finely grated zest and strained juice

1 large orange, finely grated zest and strained juice

3 passionfruit cut in half, reserve pulp

¼ cup caster sugar

⅓ cup cream

2 eggs (59g)

additional ingredients

passionfruit

whipped cream for serving

shared secrets

Pastry cases may be prepared well in advance.

The tarts are best cooked and eaten within the hour.

Whole passionfruit freeze well and defrost quickly when required.

prepare pastry.

line flan tin/s with prepared pastry. Freeze for 10-15 minutes. Pre-bake for 15-20 minutes, allow to cool before filling.

lower oven temperature to 160°C

for the filling

combine citrus juices, zest and passionfruit pulp. You will need ⅔ cup (150ml) all together.

add sugar and stir to dissolve.

whisk cream and eggs together with a whisk or use an electric mixer.

add combined liquid and blend together.

pour into pastry cases, (refer **tips on pastry making and baking - to fill pastry cases with liquid filling** page 144).

bake for 25-30 minutes or until set.

cool on a wire rack and leave for 10 minutes before removing from tin/s.

serve with extra passionfruit pulp and whipped cream.

berry jam tart with coconut topping

Serves 6

Spray or lightly grease a 23cm flan tin with removable base. Individual or mini tarts can also be prepared using this recipe.

preheat oven to 190°C

shortcrust pastry *(page 145)* or
rich nutty shortcrust pastry *(page 146)*

for the topping
50g unsalted butter

¼ cup caster sugar

1 egg (59g)

1 tablespoon maize cornflour

2 tablespoons cream

¾ cup desiccated coconut

*¼ cup stale **sponge cake** crumbs (page 63) or **butter cake** crumbs (page 47)*

1 cup berry jam or jam to your liking

additional ingredients
cream to serve (optional)

prepare pastry.

line flan tin/s with prepared pastry. Freeze for 10-15 minutes. Pre-bake for 15-20 minutes, allow to cool before filling.

for the topping

cream butter and sugar together in a food processor or electric mixer.

add egg, cornflour and cream and process until smooth. Scrape down sides and base of food processor or mixing bowl.

add coconut and cake crumbs, pulse for a few seconds to combine.

spread pastry base with jam.

spoon coconut topping over jam and spread it a little.

bake for about 15-20 minutes or until golden brown.

cool on a wire rack and leave for 10 minutes before removing from tin/s.

serve hot with cream or cold for morning or afternoon tea.

shared secrets

Pastry case may be prepared in advance.

Topping best prepared just prior to baking.

Tart will keep well for several days.

crumbly apple tart

Serve this tart straight from the dish in which it is cooked. Alternatively bake in a flan tin with removable base. Individual tarts look impressive too.

Serves 6

Spray or lightly grease a 23cm ovenproof pie dish or flan tin/s.

preheat oven to 190°C

shortcrust pastry *(page 145) or*
rich nutty shortcrust pastry
  (page 146)

for the apples
4-6 large cooking apples
1 tablespoon unsalted butter
¼ cup caster sugar (or to taste)
a small piece of cinnamon stick

for the crumble
2 tablespoons unsalted butter
2 tablespoons gluten free plain flour
2 tablespoons shredded coconut
2 tablespoons roughly chopped almonds or raw cashew nuts
2 tablespoons gluten free muesli or gluten free biscuit crumbs
2 tablespoons brown or caster sugar
½ teaspoon ground cinnamon

prepare pastry.

line dish/flan tin/s with prepared pastry. Place in freezer for 10-15 minutes. Pre-bake for 15-20 minutes. **If you are using a ceramic pie dish do not freeze the pastry before pre-baking, as the dish may crack.**

lower oven temperature to 180°C

for the apples
peel, core and cut apples into small chunks.

place butter, sugar, cinnamon and apples into a wide-based frypan.

simmer gently, turning apples occasionally until cooked but not soft.

increase heat to reduce any excess syrup in the frypan.

remove cinnamon and spoon apples into pastry shell.

for the crumble
make this by hand or in the food processor.

combine crumble ingredients working butter through with fingers.

scatter crumble over apples.

bake for about 25 minutes or until crumble turns light golden brown.

variations
1. crumbly 'appleberry' tart
Combine equal quantities of roughly chopped cooked apples (still a little crispy), blueberries and raspberries. Sprinkle with caster sugar and liqueur (optional). Top with crumble and bake as above.

2. crumbly rhubarb and apple tart
Combine cooked rhubarb and apple, apple and plum or a combination of all three. (I often cheat by using a jar of dark plums in syrup. They are available from the supermarket. Remember to remove stones from fruit and drain the syrup.) Top with crumble and bake as above.

fresh strawberry tarts

If you prepare and freeze pastry bases in advance, this is a particularly quick and easy dessert to have ready in a matter of minutes.

Serves 6

Spray or lightly grease 6 individual 8cm x 2cm flan tins with removable bases.

preheat oven to 190°C

shortcrust pastry (page 145)

cheat's custard (page 85)

2 punnets of ripe, small strawberries

for the glaze

3 tablespoons quince or redcurrant jelly

1 tablespoon water

2 teaspoons strained lemon juice

additional ingredients

whipped cream to serve

shared secrets

Pastry cases may be prepared a day in advance and stored in an airtight container.

Custard may be prepared 2 days in advance.

Dessert best assembled close to serving time.

prepare pastry.

line flan tins with prepared pastry. Freeze for 10-15 minutes. Pre-bake for 20-25 minutes, allow to cool before filling. The pastry needs to be light golden brown as it will not be baked twice.

prepare cheat's custard and cool.

rinse and hull strawberries. Pat dry on paper towel. You will require 4 strawberries per tart, 3 cut in half and 1 left whole.

to assemble the tarts

fill pastry cases with custard to within 2-3mm of the rim. Smooth with the back of a spoon.

arrange strawberry halves around edge of tart and place a whole strawberry in the centre.

place jelly, water and lemon juice in a micro-safe container and microwave on High for 1 minute.

stir, then microwave for another 30 seconds or until jelly has melted. Cool slightly.

brush glaze over berries.

serve with whipped cream.

lemon, lime and coconut tarts with passionfruit sauce

Serves 6

Spray or lightly grease a 22cm or 23cm flan tin with removable base, or alternatively 6 individual flan tins.

preheat oven to 190°C

shortcrust pastry *(page 145) or*
rich nutty shortcrust pastry *(page 146)*
passionfruit sauce *(page 41)*

for the filling
2 lemons, finely grated zest and strained juice
2 limes, finely grated zest and strained juice
½ cup caster sugar
2 eggs (59g) + 1 egg yolk
100ml coconut cream
100ml cream
2 tablespoons shredded coconut

additional ingredients
whipped cream to serve

shared secrets
Pastry cases may be prepared well in advance.

Prepare filling on the day.

Tarts are best cooked and eaten within the hour.

prepare pastry.

line flan tin/s with prepared pastry. Freeze for 10-15 minutes. Pre-bake for 15-20 minutes, allow to cool before filling.

prepare passionfruit sauce.

lower oven temperature to 160°C

for the filling
combine juice (you will require ⅓ cup of juice) and zest from lemons and limes.

add sugar and stir to dissolve. Put aside briefly.

whisk eggs, plus yolk, coconut cream and cream together.

add citrus liquid and blend together.

pour into pastry cases (refer **tips on pastry making and baking - to fill pastry cases with liquid fillings** page144).

sprinkle with coconut.

bake for 25-30 minutes or until set.

cool on a wire rack and leave for 10 minutes before removing from tin/s.

serve warm or at room temperature with passionfruit sauce and softly whipped cream.

lemon and macadamia meringue pies

Bake zesty lemon and macadamia crusted tarts. Top with meringue for a great old-fashioned favourite.

Serves 6-8

preheat oven to 180°C

**zesty lemon and macadamia
crusted tarts** *(page 161)*

for the meringue

2 eggs (59g), whites only

⅓ cup caster sugar

prepare and bake zesty lemon and macadamia crusted tarts.

for the meringue

beat egg whites until soft peaks form.

add sugar gradually, beating well until dissolved and mixture becomes glossy.

spoon meringue on top of filling and spread to the edge of pie crust.

draw mixture into peaks.

bake for 10-15 minutes or until lightly browned.

cool on a wire rack for 5 minutes before removing from tin/s.

pine nut and cumquat tart

Life's a picnic with this tart! The sweet and bitter sensation of cumquats teams perfectly with pine nuts in this tart. Not only is this a great dessert tart but perfect to take on a picnic as it will transport easily.

Spray or lightly grease a 22cm or 23cm flan tin with removable base.

preheat oven to 190°C

shortcrust pastry *(page 145)*

for the filling

80g brandied or preserved cumquats (or use a combination of both)

1 tablespoon orange liqueur

1 orange, finely grated zest only

1 lemon, finely grated zest only

75g unsalted butter

⅓ cup caster sugar

2 eggs (59g)

1 tablespoon white rice flour

1 tablespoon maize cornflour

2 tablespoons cream

½ cup dried gluten free breadcrumbs

¼ cup + ½ cup pine nuts

shared secrets

Pastry case may be prepared well in advance.

Filling best prepared just prior to baking.

This is a great tart to make in advance.

Tart can be frozen.

prepare pastry.

line flan tin with prepared pastry. Freeze for 10-15 minutes. Pre-bake for 15-20 minutes, allow to cool before filling.

lower oven temperature to 180°C

for the filling

cut brandied cumquats in halves and remove seeds.

place cumquats, liqueur and citrus zest in a food processor and puree roughly.

remove from food processor and set aside.

cream butter and sugar in a food processor until light and creamy.

add eggs one at a time.

add flours, cream, breadcrumbs and **only ¼ cup** of pine nuts and process to combine.

add reserved cumquat puree, blending well.

pour filling into pastry shell and smooth top with the back of a spoon.

sprinkle remaining pine nuts over top of tart.

bake for about 40-50 minutes until filling firms and becomes golden in colour.

cool on a wire rack and leave for at least 15 minutes before removing from tin.

pear and almond tart

Tinned pears can be used successfully in this recipe. It's okay to cheat! Buy a large tin and enjoy any remaining pears for breakfast. This is a great tart to take on a picnic!

Serves 8-10

Spray or lightly grease a 23cm flan tin with removable base. Alternatively a 10cm x 35cm rectangular flan tin may be used. (Refer - **tips on pastry making and baking pastry - to roll and press** (page 144) before lining a large flan tin with pastry.)

preheat oven to 190°C

shortcrust pastry *(page 145) or*

rich nutty shortcrust pastry *(page146)*

for the filling

1 large tin pear halves (you will need the equivalent of 3 or 4 pears, depending on the size of the pears). Alternatively, prepare and poach 3 or 4 fresh beurre bosc pears in a light sugar syrup (½ cup of sugar to 1 cup of water and a squeeze of lemon juice).

75g unsalted butter

½ cup caster sugar

a few drops of almond essence

2 eggs (59g)

1 cup ground almonds

1 cup stale gluten free **sponge cake** *crumbs (page 63) or* **butter cake** *crumbs (page 47)*

2 or 3 tablespoons apricot jam or marmalade

prepare pastry.

line flan tin with prepared pastry. Freeze for 10-15 minutes. Pre-bake for 15-20 minutes, allow to cool before filling.

lower oven temperature to 180°C

for the filling

drain pears really well on paper towel. Set aside.

cream butter, sugar and almond essence together in a food processor or electric mixer.

add eggs and beat to combine, scrape down sides of bowl.

stir in almonds and cake crumbs.

spread mixture into pastry case.

arrange drained pears (cut side down) on top of filling.

warm jam in microwave on Medium for 30 seconds or until melted.

glaze pears with warmed jam using a pastry brush.

bake for about 45-50 minutes or until filling is firm and cooked through. If tart is not quite cooked after 50 minutes, continue to cook at 160°C for about 10 minutes.

cool on a wire rack and leave for at least 15 minutes before removing from tin.

shared secrets

Substitute apricots for pears (remove stones), and glaze with warmed apricot jam.

Substitute plums for pears (remove stones), and glaze with warmed redcurrant jelly.

Pear and almond tart best eaten on the day, but it will keep well for 3-4 days. Tart may be frozen.

zesty lemon and macadamia crusted tarts

These tarts look particularly gorgeous when garnished with **glazed lemon slices** (optional). You will require 8 lemon slices for 8 tarts. But, if you are like me you will not be able to resist eating several slices before serving the tarts, therefore prepare at least 12 slices!

Serves 6-8

Spray or lightly grease a 22cm or 23cm flan tin or 8 individual 8cm x 2cm flan tins with removable bases.

preheat oven to 190°C

for the pastry

rich nutty shortcrust pastry *(page 146) substituting the nut meal with 40g roasted macadamia nuts*

for the filling

2-3 large lemons, finely grated zest and ½ cup strained juice

3 eggs (59g) + 1 yolk

½ cup caster sugar

100ml cream

additional ingredient

cream to serve

for the pastry

prepare pastry, however the first step is to place macadamia nuts into a food processor and process with several tablespoons of the flour. Add remaining flour and continue to follow the recipe.

line flan tin/s with prepared pastry. Freeze for 10-15 minutes. Pre-bake for about 15-20 minutes, allow to cool before filling. If your flan tins are deeper than 2cm the filling will be enough for 6.

lower oven temperature to 160°C

for the filling

blend lemon juice, zest, eggs plus yolk, sugar and cream in a food processor, electric mixer or by hand using a whisk.

transfer filling to a jug.

pour into pastry cases (refer **tips on pastry making and baking - to fill pastry cases with liquid fillings** page 144).

bake for 25-30 minutes or until set.

cool on a wire rack and leave for 10 minutes before removing from tin/s.

serve warm or at room temperature.

top each tart with a glazed lemon slice and serve with cream.

continued on next page

zesty lemon and macadamia crusted tarts *(continued)*

for the glazed lemon slices

1 large lemon, cut into 12 x 3mm even slices and seeds removed

boiling water

½ cup sugar

½ cup cold water

1 or 2 kaffir lime leaves

for the glazed lemon slices

place lemon slices into a bowl.

boil kettle and pour water over slices to cover.

allow to cool a little.

drain water off lemon slices.

repeat this step 3 or 4 times until bitter taste is all but gone from the water.

combine sugar, cold water and kaffir lime leaves in a frypan large enough to hold the slices in a single layer.

heat gently to dissolve sugar.

add drained lemon slices and simmer very, very gently for 1 hour or until lemon slices become shiny, translucent and the liquid syrupy. Turn slices several times during cooking.
DO NOT hurry the cooking process as the syrup and lemon slices may burn.

shared secrets

Pastry cases may be prepared well in advance.

Prepare filling on the day.

Tarts are best cooked and eaten within the hour.

Glazed lemon slices will keep well for 2 or 3 days in the refrigerator but will need to be warmed in a microwave on Medium for about 20-30 seconds to soften the toffee syrup.

kitchen equipment

baking trays

best quality knives

crepe pan, non-stick

digital scales

electric mixer or hand-held electric beater

electric knife

food processor

frypan - heavy-based

hand-held electric blender

melon baller

metal cutting shapes-square, round and oval

metric measuring cups and spoons

mixing bowls - stainless steel

moulds - timbale and dariole

ovenproof pudding moulds

piping bag - various size nozzles

ruler for measuring tins etc

saucepans - heavy based

shaker - used for dusting flour, cocoa, icing sugar etc

spatula

spoons - one large metal, one large slotted metal

scissors for cutting baking paper to fit tins etc

tins - cake, loaf, flans, friand tray, patty pan, muffin tray and springform

tongs

whisks - large and small

wire racks for cooling

wire sieve

tools used exclusively for cooking sweet food
(This is to avoid onion and garlic odours.)

chopping board

pastry brush

wooden spoons

spatula

other necessities

foil

freezer wrap (go-between)

baking paper

paper patty pans

plastic wrap

gluten & wheat free pantry stock list for recipes in this book

the gluten free symbol

An ear of wheat with a line struck through the centre is used by the Coeliac Society to protect coeliac sufferers from the risk of purchasing commercial food products containing gluten. The symbol appears on packaging with or without a circle around it.

Note: Not all packaging bears this symbol, so it is important to study the listed ingredients on all products.

almond essence
arrowroot
baking powder, gluten free
bicarbonate of soda
buckwheat flour
canned pears, plums and apples
chestnut flour
chickpea flour
chocolate: dark, light and white bits
cocoa
coconut: desiccated and shredded
coconut cream
coconut milk
cornflour (maize)
cornmeal, polenta
cream of tartar
custard powder, gluten free
dried fruits: apricots, craisins, raisins and sultanas
FG Roberts gluten free plain flour
FG Roberts gluten free self raising flour
gelatine powder

glutinous rice flour (available from Asian grocery stores)
golden syrup
grapeseed oil
honey
icing sugar, pure
jams and marmalades
jelly, gluten free
muesli, gluten free
nuts (various)
potato flour
red currant jelly
rice flour
spices, pure
sugar: granulated, caster, light and dark brown
vanilla essence or vanilla extract
vegetable oil
vinegar: white wine and balsamic
walnut oil

conversion table

for main gluten free ingredients used in this book

metric cups	grams (approx)
1 cup almonds, whole	150
1 cup almonds, ground	110
1 cup biscuit crumbs	60
1 cup breadcrumbs, dry	120
1 cup breadcrumbs, soft	60
1 cup buckwheat flour	150
1 cup butter	250
1 cup cake crumbs, stale	100
1 cup cocoa	110
1 cup coconut, desiccated	90
1 cup coconut, shredded	65
1 cup cornflour	125
1 cup custard powder	125
1 cup flour, gluten free plain and gluten free self raising	140
1 cup hazelnuts, coarse-ground	110
1 cup icing sugar	150
1 cup pine nuts	135
1 cup polenta, fine	175
1 cup potato flour	175
1 cup rice flour	175
1 cup sugar, granulated	220
1 cup sugar, caster	220
1 cup sugar, moist brown, lightly packed	155
1 cup sugar, moist brown, firmly packed	185

temperature chart

Temperatures	Celsius	Fahrenheit
Very slow	110-120	250
Slow	150	300
Moderately slow	160-180	325-350
Moderate	190-200	375-400
Moderately hot	220-230	425-450
Hot	250-260	475-500
Very hot	270-290	525-550

glossary - gluten free flours

There are a great variety of flours suitable to use in gluten free cooking. The texture of gluten free flours is fine and dense; they do not sift like wheaten flours. Use a wire sieve to sift the flour, working the flour through the mesh using your fingers or the back of a spoon.

Often more liquid is required when using gluten free flours. Err on the side of caution, adding a little at a time.

I have mainly used Roberts Gluten Free Plain and Self Raising Flour throughout this book. Their ingredients are a combination of maize starch, tapioca starch, wholegrain brown rice, wholegrain maize and soy flours.

If commercial gluten free plain and self raising flour are unavailable, success can be found by using a combination of flours such as rice flour, cornflour, soy and buckwheat. As not all flours have the same properties as one another, the texture of the finished product will vary.

I hope that the following guide to gluten free flours will be helpful. So be brave, experiment and discover new recipes for yourself, your family and friends to enjoy.

arrowroot - used to thicken sauces and custards that do not require high heat. It gives a clear, glossy finish.

brown rice flour - used in the same way as that of white rice flour but adds nutritional value to baked goods.

buckwheat flour - related to the rhubarb family, is used in a similar way to cereal grains and combines well with other flours. It is less stable than wheat flour so should be stored in the fridge or freezer. This flour is a good source of protein and fibre and is high in complex carbohydrates. It is often used for making pancakes and pikelets.

chestnut flour - has a nutty flavour and makes great crepes. This flour goes rancid quickly, so should be stored in the fridge or freezer.

chickpea flour - made from ground chickpeas and is high in protein. It has a nutty flavour and combines well with other flours.

cornflour (maize) - milled from corn and is excellent used in combination with other flours. It blends easily with liquids to thicken sauces. Choose only 100% pure cornflour for gluten free baking as some cornflours are made from wheat.

cornmeal or polenta - a flour-like cereal made from ground corn. It can be fine or coarse in texture.

glutinous rice flour - made from rice and water. It has a sticky quality and is especially useful when making gluten free pastry. It is available from Asian grocery stores.

potato flour - a heavy and starchy flour. Use potato flour combined with other flours.

rice flour - made from ground rice. It combines well with other flours and is commonly used in gluten free baking.

soy flour - has a nutty flavour and is a muddy-yellow colour. It has high nutritional value being an excellent source of protein, iron and thiamin.

index